The Allens Hill Farm Cookbook

Recipes from
Our Family to Yours

by
John Loveland

COPYRIGHT NOTICE

THE ALLENS HILL FARM COOKBOOK is copyrighted © 2010
by John Loveland and published by
Side Order Books (www.sideorderbooks.com).

All rights reserved.
No part of this book may be reproduced in any form by any electronic or mechanical means (including photocopying, recording, or information storage or retrieval) without permission in writing from the publisher. Users are not permitted to mount any part of this book on the World Wide Web.

To buy books in quantity, contact:
John Loveland at Allens Hill Farm (www.allenshillfarm.com)
3663 County Road 40, Bloomfield, NY 14469
or call 585-657-4710

Visit Allens Hill Farm on Facebook.

Book design by Anne Kiley
www.creativelinkgraphics.com

For more information about specialty publisher
Side Order Books
visit www.sideorderbooks.com or
write to: sideorderbooks@gmail.com

Printed in the United States of America.

Dedication

To my dad, John W. "Jack" Loveland.

Among the many things I learned from you
was that although life is about duty,
it is also meant to be enjoyed.

You showed me it was cool for a guy to cook.

You left us way too soon.

Acknowledgments

Life is a journey meant to be shared. For 25 years, my wife, Carolyn, has shared the ride with me. Her patience and impatience with me has made a life that has rarely been dull, and she has helped me accomplish things I never thought I would.

I also give thanks to my two children, Jennifer and Michael, who have been both inspiration and joy; Mom and Dad (both sets); my sister, Donna, for her tireless critique and corrections to my writing over the years; and, all of those who have tested our recipes and provided invaluable feedback and encouragement.

The Allens Hill Farm Cookbook

Table of Contents

Preface . . . . Page 1

How to Use This Book 5

Apple Cider Molasses 7

Words of Wisdom 11

Recipes

    The Main Event

        Breakfast 28

        Lunch 49

        Supper 54

        Dinner 92

    Side Dishes 103

Baked Goods and Desserts

   Breakfast Baked Goods 118

   Yeasted Breads 138

   Quick Breads 145

   Desserts 148

Party Food 159

Pantry Checklist 177

Ingredients Suppliers 183

Recipe Index 187

Preface

Food and cooking have been an important part of my life for as long as I can remember. Family celebrations and gatherings always seemed to revolve around food. We may not have been wealthy, but one would never have known it by the variety and abundance at our table. Whether it was a special Christmas dinner or just a late night gathering with neighbors, great food was always part of the celebration.

My mother was a fine cook. She could produce all of the 50s and 60s standards – what we now call "comfort food." Her cooking was solid, basic, and down-to-earth. It was good food and lots of it. Suppers during the week were standard meat and potatoes or casserole fare. Fridays were meatless. And the large Sunday dinner was a tradition—a roast pork, beef, or ham with a home-baked pie or cake for dessert.

My father was the adventurous one. He loved to find exotic recipes and complex preparations. He couldn't resist the temptation to add a little of this or bit of that to mother's dinner. When he did and was caught, all hell broke loose! But he couldn't help himself. He had to play with every recipe. At the holidays, he would spend a month baking hundreds of dozens of cookies to give to the friends he made as the cop who directed traffic at the main intersection in our city. He took such joy in giving away these cookies, it made me understand the sheer and simple delight that food could bring to everyone.

In fact, I was fortunate that in our family it was the men who did the interesting cooking. One of my vivid childhood memories of my mother's father was seeing him sitting at his kitchen table with a burlap sack of hickory nuts he collected while scouting for deer in the woods. He would spend hours cracking the nuts and meticulously picking out the meats to make a hickory nut cake that was beyond description. My father baked the fancy holiday breads. It was just natural to be involved and to acquire knowledge and techniques.

As I gained skill and confidence, I was encouraged to take the reins along with my sisters. I became the primary bread baker, while they handled most of the cookie production. I soon was cooking for friends and their families. It was great fun.

Though some would have thought that my future lay in the culinary arts, instead I headed off to Cornell to obtain a degree in geology. But the lure of food could not be avoided. My work/study job landed me in Sage Dining Hall. Cornell Dining was unique in collegiate dining for its high standards. We even reproduced menus several times a year from some of the finest restaurants in the country under the watchful eyes of the guest chefs. I believe I learned as much at that job as I did in my academic career. I started out as a dishwasher. Hard work earned me a position as cook's assistant, then supervisor and eventually student manager. The experience was invaluable in learning not only about cooking and restaurant management, but lifelong lessons about the realities of the working world.

My culinary skills also landed me the job as regular cook in our student apartment for three years. I applied all the tools my mother taught me about cooking good meals on a budget. It certainly made for happy apartment mates and got me out of some of the more mundane tasks involved in communal living. They considered it a very fair trade. We would create an annual blowout meal for our friends. I would pull out some of the great recipes I learned from my father and some of my own. I also discovered that a well prepared meal could be just as attractive to the right woman as a varsity letter — a very valuable lesson, indeed.

As luck would have it, the job market for aspiring geologists had dried up by the time I graduated. With student loans to repay and needing employment, I decided to use my restaurant management background. I was hired by a major full-service restaurant chain and discovered one of the lowest forms of life—the assistant manager. Serving seven thousand meals a week and working ridiculous hours in absurd conditions was an education unto itself. Sixteen years of this lifestyle took its toll personally and on my family; it was time to move on.

Despite the assistant restaurant management experience, I never lost my love for food. Cooking for my family and friends at any opportunity has always been enjoyable. I never seem to have enough shelf space for all of my cookbooks. I love to search for new recipes, especially old foods that have fallen out of favor or have been forgotten.

One afternoon while I was at a small local library, I found a book about cooking in the frontier in our area. The resourcefulness of the pioneers has always amazed me. They seemed to be able to make "something from nothing" to fill their needs. Sugar was an expensive and often unobtainable commodity on the frontier. Cooks would use whatever they found or could make. Honey and maple syrup were the most common substitutes. Most fascinating to me was the technique they used to make molasses from apple cider. It was a sweetener that was versatile and would last almost indefinitely.

The Allens Hill Farm Cookbook

I though it might be fun to try and duplicate the process. After several attempts, I was able to produce a suitable result. The apple cider molasses had a unique flavor and wonderful color. I began to use it in various recipes that called for molasses. It was a hit with family and friends. So, it began...

Before I knew it, I was sending sample batches to friends. I developed cookie and cake recipes using apple cider molasses. Feedback was great. So, it was back into the food business. Allens Hill Farm was born.

We produce apple cider molasses, apple syrups, glazes, pancake, cookie, cake and bread mixes, granola and who knows what will come next. Customers find us at farm markets, festivals, local shops, food stores and wineries, as well as our own shop and the on the Internet.

The response from our customers has been gratifying. Yet one thing they constantly ask is, "When will you produce a cookbook with your recipes?" I hope that this effort will satisfy their desires—and appetites.

Although this book contains many recipes that call for our products, it is really an accumulation of many old favorites tweaked over the years, coupled with many of my own creation. These recipes are intended to be interesting, straight-forward and reproducible by anyone with even the most basic cooking skills. I hope they will serve as a springboard for your own innovations. Perhaps they may also serve as a way to bring family and friends together to share in one of the most fundamental and universal delights: a well-prepared meal. Invite your kids, spouse and friends into the kitchen. There is such a feeling of satisfaction that comes from enjoying and sharing the wonderful results of culinary labors.

Share it!

John Loveland
Allens Hill Farm,
Spring, 2010

How to Use this Cookbook

🌿 If you are like me, you have probably already flipped through this book. (The first thing I always do before I actually read a new cookbook is to flip through and scan the recipes). Undoubtedly, you have noticed that this cookbook is organized in a non-traditional manner. Most are organized by type of recipe—meats, breads, etc. My concept is a bit different.

The Allens Hill Farm Cookbook is arranged to make it easier to put together meals and occasions. Let's face it: "what's for dinner" may be one of the most asked questions in the world. Instead of having to come up with a recipe idea, find it in a cookbook and then assemble a meal around it, this cookbook allows you to find the main course, and then select appropriate sides, desserts and even wine from suggestions made with the recipe.

The Allens Hill Farm Cookbook

Originally, "receipts," as recipes were first called, provided only bare bones information. They assumed cooks already knew basic techniques and could adapt the recipe to available ingredients. The Allens Hill Farm Cookbook gives tips on how to become comfortable using your creativity and relying less on strict adherence to specific ingredients and instructions. We also give you some interesting food science facts. These help you understand why foods behave the way they do, dispel or validate kitchen myths and just provide some fun food trivia.

Many of our recipes are perfect for involving your kids in the kitchen. They will be able to learn basic techniques and develop a love and appreciation for food. When you see these children's blocks throughout the book, it's time to get the little ones!

We are committed to using local suppliers. The Finger Lakes region of New York produces some of the finest agricultural products and wines in the nation. When appropriate, I'll suggest products and suppliers we think you'll enjoy.

So, let's get going.

What is Apple Cider Molasses?

**Allens Hill Farm
Apple Cider Molasses**
The Old Fashioned
All Natural Sweetener
"Autumn in a Jar"*

Apple cider molasses is an all natural sweetener made from pure, fresh cider pressed from New York State apples. Additive and preservative free, this fat-free sweetener has no added sugars or syrups and can be used in a variety of ways: as a replacement for other sweeteners, as a base for glazes, dressings, sauces and marinades; or simply enjoy its wonderfully unique flavor. Gourmet Magazine Weekly Online (Nov. 11, 2007) called apple cider molasses, "Smoky and tart, with deep notes of caramel and balsamic vinegar, it's far more complex than your average molasses—but it's also far more versatile."

Created by frontier cooks who couldn't find or afford sugar, apple cider molasses was made by boiling sweet cider (rescued from the men before they could turn it all into hard cider!) until it became thick and sweet. The natural acidity allowed it to be stored indefinitely at room temperature until it was used.

Don't confuse apple cider molasses with the molasses you find in your grocery store. Regular molasses is a byproduct of sugar production: molasses is what's left after all the regular sugar is extracted. Apple cider molasses is made from pure, local apple cider. It takes about one-third bushel of apples (15 pounds) to make one 12-ounce jar of molasses.

It's All About The Apples!

The same soil and climate conditions that make the Finger Lakes Region famous for its award winning wines are ideal for apple production. These apples have an amazing balance of sweetness and acidity—perfect for cider! The cider we use is pressed from apples grown in an environmentally responsible manner using IPM (Integrated Pest Management).

How Do I use Apple Cider Molasses?

There are almost no limits to how you can use apple cider molasses; we find new ideas all of the time. Be creative! Have fun!

Use In Place Of Other Sweeteners

Apple cider molasses can be used in place of sugar, honey or syrups in recipes. When using apple cider molasses, begin by using a ratio of one-quarter cup molasses to three quarter cup of sugar or other sweetener. The flavor is intense, so start slowly and increase the amount of molasses until you find the flavor balance you like.

Adjustments In Baking

Apple cider molasses has a high natural acidity. This helps to provide powerful leavening action. Half a cup of molasses and half a teaspoon of baking soda will replace about two teaspoons of baking powder in most recipes.

Other Uses

Use apple cider molasses as a base for glazes to brush on meats, seafood, poultry or desserts—its natural acidity, sweetness and complexity make it a perfect addition to dressings and marinades—or just spread it on toast, pancakes, or stir into tea.

What is Allens Hill Farm?

Allens Hill Farm is located in the stunning Bristol Hills in upstate New York. Proprietors John and Carolyn Loveland are passionate about providing the finest all-natural products made with local ingredients right on their farm.

In addition to our molasses, glazes and syrups, we make a complete line of all natural baking mixes, granolas, snack bars and our newest item, Dukkah.

The Allens Hill Farm Cookbook

Words of Wisdom: The "I can't cook" Myth

This section is devoted to the aspiring or novice cook.

Anyone can be a successful cook. Obviously, as in any endeavor, some become better than others through a combination of practice and talent. Nevertheless, the only person I've met who cannot cook is someone who does not want to cook. Most people who have told me that they can't cook, view cooking as a chore, something worse than doing the laundry or taking out the trash. Some have had a bad experience that has scared them off from trying again. If you are reading this, in all likelihood you are interested in cooking, so you have nothing to fear.

Cooking can be a great way to save money. It is easy to fall into the trap of eating out for the sake of time and convenience. If you eat out several times a week, just add up what you are spending. Then go to a supermarket and see how much food you can purchase for the same amount. Also, add up the time it takes to drive to a restaurant, get seated, served, dine, and return home. I guarantee that you can prepare and consume a great meal in the same amount of time at a fraction of the cost. I will, in a later section, provide tips on how you can really stretch your food dollars to get better quality foods at lower prices per serving.

It's rather difficult to botch a recipe, yet it happens. That's why God made trash cans (or dogs). So, expect mistakes. That's how we learn. Be bold! Hey, even the best athletes miss the ball. The important thing is that you proceed with confidence.

If you set yourself up for success, cooking can become a true pleasure. It can be a way to relax and be productive at the same time. You make others around you happy by the fruits of your efforts. Cooking is also a wonderful way to let your creative juices flow, and it can be a true social activity involving friends and family.

Like anything else, cooking requires preparation. Read the recipe carefully. Remove potential sources of frustration. Follow the instructions closely. You will be successful.

Make sure you have all the needed ingredients at hand. Professional chefs call this *"mise en place."* Loosely translated, it means, *"put in its place."* Nothing is more aggravating than being in the middle of preparing an item and realizing you are missing an ingredient. This also applies to your kitchen. Have all the necessary pans and utensils within easy reach. Having to dig through a drawer when you need that particular utensil can drive you to distraction.

Stay organized by cleaning as you go. Sometimes it can be disheartening to put a lot of effort into preparing a great meal and then have a mountain of dishes to clean at the end. In most cases, there is time to do your dishes and wipe your counters while items are cooking. It's surprising how easy it is to have a clean kitchen at the end of your labors. It is also bad form to make a mess and expect someone else to do all of your dishes. This is an excellent lesson to stress when teaching children to cook.

When baking, don't forget to turn on the oven and set it to the proper temperature. I usually set the oven first thing. This gives it a chance to preheat while preparing the recipe. It is also good to become familiar with your oven. Each one is different from another. Some run a bit hot or cool. Others bake better when the racks are in a certain position. Trial and error will help you to determine these quirks and allow you to become a master baker and roaster.

Distraction is perhaps the biggest source of cooking errors. Concentrate on the task at hand, especially when adding a series of ingredients (my typical mistake is forgetting baking powder or soda). I've learned to put an ingredient back in its home after I use it. That way, if I get a phone call or my wife asks me a question, I know if I have added it to the recipe or not.

Accurate measuring is important, especially in baking (we'll provide some tips later on). In other types of cooking, measuring is not always so critical. An extra half teaspoon of this or tablespoon of that won't be the death of a dish. Adding an extra ingredient or subtracting one is what cooking is all about. That is how you add your own flair and style to your cooking. If every chef made every item exactly the same way, there would be no need for millions of unique restaurants or thousands of variations on the same dish. Your cultural heritage, availability of local ingredients, season of the year or what happens to be in your kitchen cupboard all influence the final product. That is as it should be.

In practice, it is typically quite difficult to over- or undercook a dish to inedibility. If you have a good kitchen timer and instant-read thermometer, it is almost impossible to fail. Experience will teach you how to use all of your senses to check for proper doneness. Aroma, color, resistance to touch or even the sound in the pan can reveal when your dish has reached the point of perfection.

Presentation is an often overlooked part of the experience. I am truly guilty myself in that I rarely, except at holidays, make much of an effort to arrange and display dishes attractively. The old saying that people eat with their eyes as well as their mouths is true. Restaurants make a fortune charging higher prices for food that has fantastic presentation. A couple of extra minutes to add garnish or just place food on an attractive plate can really make a difference.

One last bit of advice. Take the time to enjoy the food you prepare. All too often we try to cram food into our mouths when we are off to a soccer game, boy scouts or whatever. We can't always change our lives, but we can try to set aside the time to enjoy a well prepared meal on a regular basis.

Okay, I'll get off my soapbox.

If you are an aspiring cook and you want to start off slowly, look for the recipes with this children's blocks symbol. These are recipes that are perfect to learn basic techniques and build confidence.

Teach Your Children Well

I think it is unconscionable when children cannot cook for themselves. Every child should have a repertoire of basic foods that they can prepare on their own or with minimal supervision. This is important in several respects. It develops independence; it is an important survival skill they will need someday when they begin to live on their own; it allows them to contribute to the family; it frees the parents from having to get every meal; it is a springboard to teach them other life skills—doing dishes, laundry, cleaning and organizing, shopping, proper nutrition—and it develops self confidence and appreciation.

In this cookbook, many recipes are designated with a this blocks symbol. These recipes are perfect for children to learn basic cooking skills.

Involve your kids in your cooking. You'll be amazed at how much they pick up just by observing. Let them stir mixes and learn how to scrape a bowl (then let them lick the beater or spatula as a reward). Make it fun. Show them not to be afraid of an oven, how to handle hot pans safely, how to use the stove (and the dishwasher) and a knife properly.

As an added benefit, children that know how to cook will eat healthier foods. If they can make a scrambled egg, chances are they will find it's better than a pop tart or sugary cereal. A slice of a healthy whole grain quick bread beats a rice crispy treat. If they want a treat, they can make a pan of brownies themselves for the whole family to enjoy. They will learn not to depend on fast food or something from the freezer they can just microwave. This can save you a lot of money in your food budget and teach them how to do the same when they are out on their own.

Children should be able to provide breakfast and lunch for themselves. As they progress there is no reason they cannot begin to make simple dinners. Think of the time that this can free up for a parent while it also teaches responsibility and teamwork.

Kitchen Economy

It is possible to eat well on a budget. There are a number of ways to stretch your food dollars. Let me list a few tips.

Eat in not out: the cost of one dinner out could buy you groceries for a week.

Avoid frozen prepared foods: you pay a premium for these items; often they are not good quality; they also tend to be full of additives, preservatives and salt.

Buy in bulk: warehouse stores can be a great source of high quality foods at very good prices. The downside of bulk buying is learning how to manage the larger quantities. You will need some freezer and pantry space, and freezer bags. There is some time involved in cutting a pork loin into chops or splitting a six-pound package of hamburger into one pound bags. But if you are willing to do so, the savings can be significant.

Shop at local farm markets and roadside stands: they can be amazing sources of high quality foods at very reasonable prices. Check out the markets in your area. Better yet, establish relationships with the vendors you like. Farm markets are also a wonderful way to add variety with the many unique items often found there. They are a great source for organic items. See **Farmer's Market Bounty** on page 24 for great tips on how to take advantage of what the markets have to offer.

Control waste by shopping frequently for perishable items like fresh produce. Buying lettuce when its bundled "three for..." is not a value if you waste a head because you can't use it before it goes bad. The same is true with meats. Monitor your refrigerator daily. Adjust your menu planning to make sure you use up perishable items before they go bad. Check expiration dates to make sure you rotate non perishable and frozen items to use the oldest first.

Portion control saves money. Prepare reasonably sized meals to keep leftovers to a minimum (unless you are purposely cooking ahead). It seems to always be a struggle to use up leftovers, not to mention the storage issues in the fridge, and since leftovers are inevitable, we will discuss the many ways to use them in detail later in the book.

Finally, there is no shame in checking out the day-old rack. If you are going to use an item quickly, does it matter if it's close to the sell by date? My local market puts out all of its meat markdowns first thing in the morning, so I try to get there early. I often find some great values.

Kitchen Science

An understanding of the chemistry of cooking can be both interesting and instructive. When appropriate, I've included interesting facts for certain recipes or chapters. This book also exposes some old wives tales as pure bunk, while others are pure genius. If this topic is interesting to you, check out Harold McGee's book **On Food and Cooking**. It is an amazingly detailed and informative read.

Ingredients

It is simple. Better ingredients will yield better results. However, for everyday cooking, how much should you invest in your ingredients? That is a question you must answer based on your budget and your palate. For special recipes, you may want to invest in special ingredients; splurge on a real vanilla bean for homemade ice cream or fresh veal for Veal Parmesan.

Sometimes it is more economical to invest in better ingredients if by doing so you use less. Otherwise, most items you find in your favorite grocery store are just fine. In fact, I encourage you to try some of the store's own brand items. I have found that many of these are superior in quality to many name brands and are less expensive.

In the **Ingredients Suppliers** section (page 181), we list some sources for ingredients. These include spices, produce, meat, flours and specialty items.

Develop good local sources. There is an advantage in getting to know a local butcher or baker. Your town may have a great sausage maker or ethnic deli. Check out the local farm markets. Great ingredients don't have to be more expensive. Besides, buying local is a great way to support your neighbors.

Butter vs. Margarine

There is always a debate about butter versus margarine. As far as I am concerned there is simply no substitute for butter in cooking. If for health or cost factors you want to substitute margarine, shortening or another product by all means do so. However, flavor and results may differ.

Each product has different characteristics that influence its performance. Like anything else, all things in moderation. For most of us, moderate use of butter will not adversely affect our health.

Animal Fats

Sometimes lard or bacon fat is just the ticket. For instance, a piecrust made with butter or shortening simply cannot compare with one made with lard or bacon fat. The smoky flavor of bacon fat is great in a stew and allows for better browning than oil or shortening.

Fresh Herbs vs. Dried

In most instances, fresh herbs are preferable to dry. Yet, fresh herbs are certainly more expensive (unless you grow some yourself!) and are perishable. Therefore, as a cook you must make a value judgment. In most recipes, the dried herbs are just fine. However, in some dishes, say a fresh salsa, fresh cilantro is a must. My suggestion is grow your own. Many herbs are very easy (and fun) to grow. They can be raised successfully indoors in pots if you don't have a yard. If you do, set aside part of a flower bed or garden for herbs. It's wonderful to be able to go out and snip some fresh parsley or dill for a summer dish.

Fresh vs. Frozen

Another ongoing debate is whether fresh is better than frozen. If you aren't really sure about the source of fresh meats or especially seafood, go with frozen.

Let's use seafood as an example. When fish is caught in the ocean, it is usually processed and frozen onboard ship or iced until it is unloaded at port. The frozen product is frozen within hours of being caught, preserving its quality. A "fresh" fish may be several days old before it gets to the consumer steadily losing quality every minute. The same can be true of meats and poultry.

Flours

Flours come in many varieties. Most home cooks use all-purpose exclusively, with fine results. Our recipes recommend different flours for different applications. Although all-purpose flour will still provide a satisfactory result, using the specified flour will produce a noticeable difference.

Bread: high in protein, milled from hard wheat to facilitate gluten formation.

All-purpose: a medium-protein flour which will work in most applications.

Pastry: soft wheat flour low in protein for flaky piecrusts, pastries and cookies.

Cake: low in protein for dense, delicate crumb in cakes.

Mixes

Let's be real. As much as we would always like to cook from scratch, it just isn't practical. At Allens Hill Farm, we make a wide variety of high quality baking mixes. If you have limited time, grab a good quality mix. Have to make a quick supper? Stove top stuffing mix can help you whip up a quick meal. Use your creativity to spice up a mix to make it your own.

Food Safety

More people get food borne illnesses from home prepared foods than from restaurants. Unfortunately, most of us never receive any kind of education in proper food handling. A few simple tips can eliminate the majority of problems.

For more detailed information, check out **www.homefoodsafety.org**.

Temperature Control

Keep hot food hot and cold food cold. Hot food should be kept above 140°F; cold food below 40°F.

Invest in an instant-read probe thermometer. It is quite simply your best defense against food borne illness. It is also absolutely the best way to determine that food has been cooked to proper doneness to eliminate food borne pathogens (165°F).

Cooked vs. Raw (Cross Contamination)

When cooked food comes into contact with food that is uncooked or is put on a surface where raw food has been or is handled with utensils used on raw foods, the chance of contamination exists.

Never put cooked food on a plate that had raw meat on it. Always wash and sanitize cutting boards, countertops and utensils after preparing raw meats, poultry or seafood. Always wash fresh fruits and vegetables; bacteria can be present.

An often overlooked procedure is to make sure that foods are stored properly in your refrigerator. Cooked foods should always be stored above raw. If not, juices containing bacteria from raw foods can drip down onto cooked foods.

Make sure raw poultry is always on the bottom shelf, even below raw meats and seafood.

Hand Washing

One of the leading sources of food-borne illnesses comes from lack of proper hand washing. Wash hands before touching food and especially after using the bathroom. Always wash hands between the handling of raw and cooked foods.

A Well-Stocked Pantry

Keeping an inventory of the ingredients which you commonly use will make cooking a lot more enjoyable. If you know what you have on hand, you will be prepared to make just about any recipe. Just like a painter who has all the colors on the palate, a well-stocked pantry gives you flexibility to create and saves you the time of having to run to the store for a missing ingredient.

Our **Pantry Checklist** starts on page 175. You must adjust this list for your needs and tastes, but it will provide a good starting point.

Basic Utensils

You don't need to break the bank on the best cookware to be a good cook. I prefer some of the less expensive pans to the top of the line selections. You can find some great bargains. Just keep your eyes open for sales. Warehouse and discount stores often have great pans and utensils for great prices. I also love to go to restaurant supply stores. Commercial grade utensils and pans are often not much more that what you find in a department store, but are vastly superior. Let me make a quick list of some kitchen essentials.

Pans

For the stovetop, I recommend a large, medium and small non-stick sauté pan. You can often find inexpensive sets. The non stick coating doesn't last forever anyway, so don't spend a lot.

A 10-inch cast iron fry pan is great since it can go from stove top to oven. It holds heat well and can actually add iron to your diet. A cast iron Dutch oven is also handy, but not essential.

Small, medium and large saucepans are a must. Look for ones with heavy bottoms and lids. Stainless steel is preferable.

A large stockpot is great for soups, pasta, chili, etc. A griddle is more convenient than a fry pan for pancakes and grilled sandwiches. A grill pan is a nice addition to your collection when weather precludes the use of the outdoor grill. Don't forget a wok.

A roasting pan with a rack is a must.

I advise against cookie sheets. Spend a bit more on commercial half-sheet pans. They are larger, sturdier, hold heat better and last forever.

I also like commercial cake pans. Two 9-inch pans are excellent.

You should have a couple of loaf pans, muffin tins, and pie tins.

An 8-inch square cake pan and 13x9-inch pan are essential. If you have a bundt pan that's also good.

For more advanced baking consider a tube pan, a spring form pan and tart pan.

Bowls

It is amazing how many bowls you can use when you really get cooking. A mixing bowl set is a must. Two is better. Be sure they can be used in the oven if necessary. Many come with lids, which is a plus. A colander is also essential for straining and washing foods.

Utensils

Knives are the most important utensils. Invest in a good 8- or 10-inch chef's knife. Find one that feels good in your hand. Get a steel to keep it sharp. A boning knife and carving knife should also be of good quality. A paring knife is a must, but don't spend a lot on this. A cheap serrated bread knife is fine, but you do need one.

My wife recently gave me a set of ceramic knives. They are interesting and have some advantages; most notably they stay very sharp. However, they are expensive, have some limitations and require being sent out for a specialty, professional sharpening.

There are thousands of kitchen utensils. There is a gadget for every conceivable task. You need only a few:

Ladle *Timer*
Grater *Hot pads*
Rolling pin *Pizza cutter*
Cake tester *Pastry brush*
Cutting board *Potato masher*
Slotted spoon *Vegetable brush*
Probe thermometer *Set of wooden spoons*

Spatulas (turners) metal large and small
Wire whisks, at least a couple in different sizes
Tongs – two good commercial pairs, one long and one short
Spatulas (scraping) plastic heat resistant in assorted sizes

Optional but handy:

Scale
Funnel
Mandolin
Dough scraper

Appliances

A large, heavy-duty stand mixer is a must and should be the first kitchen appliance that you purchase. I invested in a Kitchen Aid nearly twenty years ago and it is still going strong despite years of heavy use. It's the best money I ever spent. There is no substitute for its ability to knead bread dough, mix cookie dough, stir cake batter and whip cream effortlessly. It will also accept a variety of attachments for everything from juicing and milling to making pasta.

A food processor would be my next choice. It is a great time saver and has dozens of applications

A heavy duty blender is great for mixing frozen drinks, making baby food and fruit smoothies.

A meat grinder is fun tool. I love to make sausage. You can have a lot of fun and save a lot of money grinding your own meats.

An ice cream maker is lots of fun. If you have one which uses a bowl which you keep in the freezer, ice cream or sorbet is ready in minutes.

Farmer's Market Bounty

In many parts of the world, people go to markets daily. What they eat depends on what they find at the market that day. Diets are driven by seasonality and growing conditions. Freshness and flavor is maximized. Building a rapport with vendors becomes a way of getting great food and suggestions. Not to mention, it's a true community event.

During the farmer's market season, there is no better way to put together a great evening meal than by making a trip to your local farmer's market. Not only will you find the freshest, locally grown products, but you'll be surprised at how the variety of goods will stimulate your creativity. As an added bonus, chances are you'll also find great values for your dollar.

As farmer's markets grow in popularity, local producers bring an ever greater variety of items to market, providing an opportunity to experience everything from heirloom vegetables to free-range meats to amazing specialty foods. The best thing is that the vendors have great ideas on how to use their products. Many even have recipes to hand out.

This is an outstanding way to introduce your family to new tastes and better nutrition. By all means, TAKE YOUR KIDS! Farmer's markets are such a fun way for them to learn about where our foods come from and how they look before they get to the plate. Many vendors have samples to taste. Chances are, they'll also meet friends there who have come with their folks.

Here are a few tips on getting the most for your dollar and finding the best products.

Get To The Market Early (But Not Too Early)

Vendors have a limited amount of product they can bring to a market. This is driven not only by the size of their crop, but by the size of their vehicle and stall space. If you go to the market too late, they may be sold out, especially if you are looking for in demand products or if it is early or late in the growing season. Therefore, get to the market as close to the opening time as possible.

However, please don't arrive before the market opens. Many markets prohibit sales before the "opening bell" (some markets actually do ring an opening bell). It is also inconsiderate to vendors who are trying to set up their stalls. If you come early, use it as a chance to see what is at the market that day.

Look Before You Buy

The smart farm market shopper begins by walking the market to see what is available that day. Typically, many farmers may have the same type of products in season. Though prices usually stay within a fairly narrow range from vendor to vendor, quality and size vary. So walk the whole market, find what you are looking for, check prices and quality then go back and make your purchases.

Try Before You Buy

You will find a lot of unfamiliar products at a good farmer's market. Most good vendors will actively sell these products by talking about them and giving samples. Again, ask questions and ask for samples. However, be considerate. Don't make the market your buffet dinner.

Get To Know Your Vendors

If there is one word of advice I have to someone who regularly goes to a particular market, it is: get to know your vendors. Establishing a rapport is the best way to understand what you are buying, get usage suggestions, and to learn all sorts of fascinating information. Many vendors will also take orders for regular customers.

A tomato is not a just a tomato. The range of options can be staggering in a good farmer's market. Is it grown using certified organic methods, just chemical free or grown using conventional farming methods? Is it an heirloom variety? Is it grown in a hot house, a hoop house or field grown? When was it picked? Is it picked ripe and ready to eat, or under-ripe?

The only way to find out is to ask a lot of questions from each vendor.

Once you get to know who's who, what they grow and how they grow it, you can determine what you want. This is where price versus quality comes into play. An organic, heirloom tomato should be more expensive than your basic tomato.

Every vendor has a story to tell. You'll be amazed at the number of vendors who have advanced degrees and amazing work experiences who instead decided to follow their passion.

If you like to garden, vendors can be an incredible source of information. They love to share their knowledge. Many are incredible cooks who can give you tremendous ideas on how to use their products.

Feel Good, Buy Local, Be a Locavore

Spending your food dollars at your local farmer's market helps to support local farms and small family businesses. These are your neighbors who work hard to support their families and provide you with great food to enjoy with your family and friends.

Keeping your dollars in your community is a great way to assure the businesses stay viable and will be there for you to purchase from in the future.

The Main Event:
Entrees and Main Courses

The first part of planning almost every meal is deciding on the main course.

The entrée is typically the most substantial and expensive part of the meal. It sets the theme for the appetizers, sides, desserts and wine choices.

This also applies to breakfast and lunch.

Breakfast Is Good – For You

Breakfast is the most ignored and least appreciated of our meals. The reason for that: most of our lives are too full and fast paced to take the time to prepare and eat a proper breakfast. The advent of cold cereals and ready-to-eat breakfast items has all but eliminated a full breakfast from most of our routines. If we do have a hot morning meal, it is either bacon-and-eggs between an English muffin from a drive-thru or a bowl of insipid oatmeal out of the microwave. The only real breakfast of the week may be Sunday, but even that custom fades.

In the early, largely rural days of our country, breakfast was typically served after morning chores were completed and the farmers had developed an appetite. Early settlers usually breakfasted on cornmeal mush or cornbread and whatever types of seasonal fruits, vegetables and meats were available. As time went on, and farms became more prosperous, more traditional breakfast foods became common: sourdough pancakes, eggs, biscuits and all types of meats, milk and coffee.

Over time as prosperity continued, and influences from immigrant food traditions impacted breakfast, fancy sweet breads and cakes were added to breakfast menus. Improved kitchen technology allowed for easier and more consistent baking—with far less effort as oven design advanced.

As lives became busier, breakfast was consumed first thing in the morning before school or work. As more women entered the workforce, particularly during and after World War II, the advent of cold prepared cereal and the toaster signaled the death of breakfast as it once was. Now most people who eat a true hot breakfast do so in a restaurant, not at home.

Most of us will never have the time to prepare a full breakfast every day. Besides, our waistlines and cholesterol levels would not allow it. That doesn't mean, however, that occasionally and as time permits, we cannot enjoy some of those traditional and wonderful breakfast foods. The best part is that we don't have to eat them just at breakfast. Some of the favorite suppers at our home include pancakes or waffles, bacon or sausage, eggs, home fries and fresh fruits.

Many breakfast foods are simple, quick and easy to prepare. They are a great way to introduce children to cooking. They are also economical for those on a budget. Yet, some of the following recipes allow us to be indulgent and create marvelous pastries. Make time for breakfast foods. They are good…and good for you.

**Allens Hill Farm
8 Grain Buttermilk
Pancake Mix**

 # Hot Off The Griddle

There is something about pancakes, waffles and French toast that says "family meal". They are true comfort foods often shared as a weekend ritual or at family or holiday gatherings—and don't forget that they are great supper items for an economical change of pace.

These foods take us back to our roots as a nation where flapjacks and griddlecakes were consumed in enormous quantities by farmers, lumberjacks and laborers who built our country decades ago.

Pancakes, waffles and French toast are great foods for kids or novice cooks to learn basic cooking skills. Once they have mastered the tools it takes to make a pancake, can an omelet be far behind?

Making these foods from scratch is practically as easy as using a store bought mix and the final product is so much better (unless you're using one of Allens Hill Farm's mixes, of course). Let's get mixin' and flippin'!

Pancakes

Quick and easy to fix, pancakes still are a weekend tradition in many American households. Most stick to the convenience of prepared mixes. There are many fine ones on the market, including our own Allens Hill Farm brand. The following recipes provide you with some basic styles and variations. Pancakes are easy to experiment with, so develop your own combination of flours and additions of fruits and spices.

Why are buttermilk pancakes so popular and considered by many to be superior? It's a simple matter of chemistry. Chemical leavenings require acid to produce a reaction that releases carbon dioxide during the cooking process. It is the bubbles of carbon dioxide that puff up a pancake. Baking powder is a combination of chemicals, essentially baking soda and an acid that react when liquid is added to the ingredients. Baking soda reacts directly with the acidic ingredients in the recipe to produce the gas bubbles.

Since buttermilk is quite acidic, it does an excellent job of producing prodigious amounts of carbon dioxide in reaction to the baking soda. Therefore, it tends to produce a lighter and fluffier pancake. If you don't have buttermilk, there are other tricks you can use. Sour milk will also achieve the same effect. Since most don't have sour milk on hand, simply stir a tablespoon of lemon juice or white vinegar to a cup of milk and let sit about 15 minutes.

A number of other items are acidic as well: sour cream, yogurt, fresh fruit, honey, molasses and even cocoa. The addition of a cup of any of these requires an adjustment to the amount of leavening used. Rule of thumb is to decrease the amount of baking powder by two teaspoons and increase the baking soda by one-half teaspoon.

Pancakes are one of the best ways to introduce kids to using a stovetop. Pancake mix is simple to make, so a novice cook can easily complete the process from start to finish. Be sure to review safety tips with your particular style of stove; each has its dangers be it gas, electric, induction, etc. Teach them that a stove should be respected, not feared. Yet, also tell them what to do if they do burn themselves.

Explain how to test a pan to see if it is hot enough to cook with. Dropping beads of water on a hot griddle demonstrates the visual and auditory aspects of cooking. As they cook the pancakes, kids learn the cues to tell them when to flip the pancake and how to adjust the heat to obtain the desired results each and every time. Don't forget to reinforce with them to clean up as they go and to do the dishes afterwards. Be sure to monitor and supervise until both of you are comfortable and confident. You'll be surprised at how soon your kids will be fixing breakfast for themselves and for you.

Pancakes

This is the most basic of pancake recipes and known by many names: flapjacks, griddlecakes, string of flats, flatcars… It is made with milk and all-purpose flour. There are several suggested variations as well. Don't be afraid to be creative. This recipe will feed 4–6, so double or triple as company dictates. If you are cholesterol conscious, reduce to one egg or even eliminate.

> 2 eggs
> 2 cups all-purpose flour
> 4 teaspoons baking powder
> 0–4 tablespoon sugar
> 1 teaspoon salt
> 1-1/2–2 cups milk
> 2 tablespoons oil or melted butter

In a large mixing bowl, beat eggs and whisk in milk and oil. Adjust amount of milk to make a thinner or thicker batter as you prefer. Mix dry ingredients in a separate bowl. The amount of sugar is optional. It is not a required ingredient. Add to liquid and stir until just mixed. Don't over stir or the pancake will be tough. A few lumps are okay. The batter will thicken as it sits. Add more milk if needed.

Heat a lightly greased frying pan or griddle over medium to medium high heat until a few drops of water will dance and sputter when dropped on it. Ladle or spoon two tablespoons to one-quarter cup of batter onto the pan depending on how large you like your pancakes. Cook until bubbles form and burst on top of the pancake. Flip and cook for a minute or two on the other side.

Pancakes should be a golden brown and cooked through; if not, adjust the heat of the pan and cooking time until you are producing a consistent pancake. Re-grease the pan as needed. Once you get it right, you should be able to cook up the batch to perfection in no time. If necessary, keep pancakes warm in a low oven until served.

Serve warm with butter, maple syrup, Allens Hill Farm Apple syrups or honey.

Makes 4–6 servings.

Variations

Whole Wheat: use one cup of whole wheat flour and one cup all-purpose.

Blueberry: add one cup of fresh blueberries to the finished batter. If using dried berries, one-quarter cup is plenty. Soak in boiling water to re-hydrate first.

Buckwheat: use one cup of buckwheat flour and one cup all-purpose.

Chocolate Chip: add three-quarters of a cup of chocolate chips to the batter; use a bit less milk—a thicker batter works best here.

Apple Cinnamon: peel, core and chop one apple; add to batter with one-half teaspoon of cinnamon—this is better with the four tablespoons of sugar in the mix.

🌾 Multigrain: use just about any types of flours you choose; just keep the all-purpose proportion at about 50%, and use whatever you like for the other—oat, corn, buckwheat, graham, soy, rice, potato all work well.

🌾 High Fiber: add a couple of tablespoons of oat bran, wheat bran, wheat germ to any of the variations to make a higher fiber version.

🌾 Waffles: cook batter in a waffle iron to make great, easy waffles.

🌾 Buttermilk Pancakes 🌾

This recipe is essentially identical to the previous except for the use of buttermilk in place of regular milk and the addition of baking soda. Dried buttermilk powder can be used in place of buttermilk with excellent results. This can be found in most grocery stores. Simply add one-half cup of buttermilk powder to the dry ingredients and use water in place of the buttermilk. If you are cholesterol conscious, reduce to one egg or eliminate the egg.

2 eggs	1 teaspoon salt
0–4 tablespoon sugar	2 cups all-purpose flour
1 teaspoon baking soda	1-1/2–2 cups buttermilk
1 teaspoon baking powder	2 tablespoons oil or melted butter

In a large mixing bowl, beat eggs and whisk in buttermilk and oil. Adjust amount of buttermilk to make a thinner or thicker batter as you prefer. Mix dry ingredients in a separate bowl. The amount of sugar is optional. It is not a required ingredient. Add to liquid and stir until just mixed. Don't over stir or the pancake will be tough. A few lumps are okay. The batter will thicken as it sits, add more milk if needed.

Heat a lightly greased frying pan or griddle over medium to medium high heat until a few drops of water will dance and sputter when dropped on it. Ladle or spoon two tablespoons to one-quarter cup of batter onto the pan depending on how large you like your pancakes. Cook until bubbles form and burst on top of the pancake. Flip and cook for a minute or two on the other side.

Pancakes should be a golden brown and cooked through. If not adjust the heat of the pan and cooking time until you are producing a consistent pancake. Re-grease the pan as needed. Once you get it right, you should be able to cook up the batch to perfection in no time. If necessary, keep pancakes warm in a low oven until served.

Serve warm with butter, maple syrup, Allens Hill Farm Apple syrups or honey.

Makes 4–6 servings.

Variations

🌾 See all of the variations above for pancakes: these are all perfectly acceptable to use with buttermilk pancakes.

Make Your Own Buttermilk Pancake Mix

🌾 To save time, you can make your own pancake mix. Nothing is simpler. All you need is dried buttermilk powder.

In a large bowl, triple the dry ingredients found in the recipe above. Add one-and-a-half cups of dried buttermilk powder. Stir well and place in a sealed container or Ziploc bag. When ready to use, measure out two cups of mix. Add one-and-a-half to two cups of water, one egg and/or two tablespoons of oil and stir.

🌾 Cornmeal Pancakes 🌾

The original American griddlecakes were commonly known as johnnycakes. They were simply cornmeal and salt cooked in boiling water to make a porridge or pudding. This was then cooked on a hot griddle. Our version is a bit more sophisticated and palatable.

1 egg	1 cup milk
2 tablespoons oil	1/2 teaspoon salt
1 cup all-purpose flour	3/4 cup yellow cornmeal
4 teaspoons baking powder	2 tablespoons sugar, or to taste

Mix dry ingredients in a bowl. Add remaining ingredients and stir. This batter is better a bit thick. Cook on a hot griddle. Cool any leftover cakes on a rack. They are excellent the next day toasted.

Makes 4 servings.

Variation

🌾 Use Allens Hill Farm Apple Cider Molasses in place of sugar.

🌾 Sourdough Pancakes 🌾

Sourdough pancakes are a very old-fashioned fare. When my father grew up on a farm, pancakes were made from starter. Sourdough pancakes have a distinctive taste that is, as the name implies a bit sour. Starter is kept refrigerated, kind of in a state of suspended animation, until ready to use. When it is put into a warm place it comes to life.

Some bakers claim to have kept a starter alive for decades. As a living thing, it needs to be fed and cared for. We will start with the starter, then explain how to use it to make amazingly unique pancakes.

Starter

There are as many different ways to create a starter as there are bakers. Thousands of years ago, starters were created from the natural yeasts found in the air. Modern starters can be made using modern yeasts or by fermentation caused by microbes present in buttermilk.

We will use a yeast starter. Creating the starter takes a few days, but once you have it, as long as you feed it and care for it, it will go on indefinitely.

1/2 teaspoon salt
1 tablespoon yeast
2 cups lukewarm water
2 cups all-purpose flour

Mix the ingredients together in a bowl. Let batter sit in a warm place in the kitchen. For the next four days, add an additional one-half cup of flour and one-half cup of warm water each day to feed it. It is now ready to use. If you plan to use it later, add additional flour and water, and refrigerate. Try to keep it in the least cool part of the refrigerator. The starter should be fed at least once a week by adding flour and water.

When using the starter, always replace what is taken with equal amounts of flour and water mixture (if two cups of starter are removed, add one cup water and one cup flour). Do not let the starter be contaminated by oil or eggs.

Pancakes

The night before you plan to make the pancakes, put two cups of starter in a bowl. Add one cup of flour and one cup of warm water. Mix together and let sit in a warm place covered over night. By morning it should be nice and bubby.

Take two cups of this mixture and put in a bowl for your pancakes. The other two cups will be used to put it back into the starter in the fridge.

1 cup milk   *2 cups starter*
3 eggs, beaten   *1-1/2 cups flour*
1/4 teaspoon salt   *0–4 tablespoons sugar*
1/2 teaspoon baking soda *1/4 cup oil or melted butter*
1 tablespoon baking powder

Add milk, eggs and oil to starter. Mix together dry ingredients and stir into wet ingredients.

Let batter sit for several minutes.

Cook pancakes on hot griddle.

Makes 4 to 6 servings.

Old Fashioned Buckwheat Cakes

These are a very old fashioned pancake made with buckwheat and yeast. They must be started the night before.

2 cups milk
1/2 teaspoon salt
1-1/2 teaspoons yeast
2 cups buckwheat flour
1 teaspoon baking soda
1/4 cup lukewarm water
1 tablespoon Allens Hill Farm Apple Cider Molasses or regular molasses

Scald milk. Put in a mixing bowl and let cool to lukewarm. Mix yeast with water to dissolve. Add to milk and add buckwheat and salt. Beat well for a couple of minutes. Cover with a cloth and let sit at room temperature overnight.

The next morning, stir in remaining ingredients and about one-quarter cup of warm water or enough to achieve the proper consistency. Cook on a hot griddle.

Makes 4 to 6 servings.

Crepes

Crepes are simple and versatile. They can be used for any meal or dessert.

2 eggs
1 cup milk
1/2 teaspoon salt
1 cup all-purpose flour
2 tablespoons melted butter

Beat eggs in a bowl. Whisk in milk, butter, flour and salt. Cover and let sit for 30 minutes or more. Heat a 7- or 8-inch crepe pan or non-stick skillet moderately hot. Pour in a small amount of batter and tilt and swirl the pan until the batter covers the bottom. Return to the heat and cook until edges just start to curl and dry. Flip and cook the other side for a minute more. Remove from pan and put on plate.

Cook remaining batter. Re-grease pan as necessary.

Makes 12 to 15 crepes.

Variation

Buckwheat Crepes: use one-half cup all-purpose flour and one-half cup buckwheat flour.

🌾 CREPES WITH EGGS 🌾

eggs (2 per person)
prepared crepes (2 per person—recipe on page 36)
shredded cheese (Swiss, gruyere, cheddar, or your favorite)
breakfast meat cooked (thinly sliced ham, bacon, or crumbled sausage)

Preheat oven to 400°F. Scramble eggs and cook until done, but still moist (see recipe page 43). Put a crepe on a buttered baking sheet, darker side down. Place a slice of ham or bacon on crepe. Add one scrambled egg, a sprinkle of cheese and a sprinkle of pepper if desired. Roll up and place seam side down on pan. When all crepes are rolled up, place in oven and bake about 5 minutes. Serve immediately.

Variation
Use any of your favorite omelet fillings (mushrooms, peppers, asparagus, and onions) and add to the scrambled eggs. You may omit the meat, if desired, as well as the cheese.

Waffles

Waffles are a wonderful alternative to pancakes. Essentially the same batter can be cooked in a waffle iron. If you are used to the insipid frozen waffles heated in a toaster, you must try the real thing. Waffles can also be made with a sweeter batter and are great as a base for desserts.

🌾 MOM'S GOLDEN WAFFLES 🌾

There are many waffle recipes, but my favorite is the one my mother made. I have yet to find one better. The key is the egg whites that make the waffles very light and fluffy.

1/3 cup oil *1-1/4 cups milk*
1/4 teaspoon salt *2 eggs, separated*
2 tablespoons sugar *2 cups all-purpose flour*
1 tablespoon baking powder

Mix together dry ingredients. In a mixing bowl beat egg yolks and add milk and oil. In another bowl, beat egg whites stiff. Add dry ingredients to milk mixture and stir until smooth. Gently fold in egg whites. Bake in waffle iron.

Makes 4 to 6 servings.

❦ Belgian Waffles ❦

Belgian waffles are great for desserts, but they can just as well be eaten for breakfast. They are yeast raised, sweet and rich with the flavor of vanilla.

>2 cups milk 1/4 cup sugar
>1/2 cup butter 1/2 teaspoon salt
>2 egg yolks, beaten 2 teaspoons vanilla
>1/2 teaspoon sugar 1 tablespoon yeast
>1/2 cup warm water 1/2 teaspoon nutmeg
>2-1/2 cup all-purpose flour

Scald milk. Place in large bowl with sugar, butter and salt and let cool to lukewarm. Add yeast and one-half teaspoon of sugar to warm water. Whisk eggs and vanilla into milk. Stir in flour and nutmeg. Beat to form a smooth batter. Cover and let rise for an hour. Beat down and cook in waffle iron. Serve warm with butter and syrup or top with ice cream, whipped cream, hot fudge or fruit toppings.

Makes 6 to 8 waffles (depending on the size of your waffle iron).

❦ French Toast ❦

French toast is also called pain perdu, French for lost bread, since French toast was intended as a way to avoid wasting stale bread. It still is better made with stale bread. Just about any bread will do. The better the bread the better the French toast. French bread, Italian bread, challah, raisin bread are all great resources. One-inch-thick slices are optimal.

This recipe is good for about four servings. If you need to increase or decrease, figure one egg per serving and adjust the other ingredients accordingly. This recipe is sweet and rich, almost like a custard. If you prefer, omit the sugar and vanilla.

>4 eggs 1 cup milk
>1/4 teaspoon salt 2 tablespoons sugar
>1 teaspoon vanilla 8 slices stale bread
>1/2 teaspoon cinnamon 1/4 teaspoon nutmeg

Whisk all ingredients, except bread, together in a bowl. Heat a greased griddle medium hot, like for pancakes. Dip slices of bread in egg mixture to coat both sides. Cook on griddle until golden brown on both sides. Serve warm with butter, syrup or cinnamon sugar.

Makes 4 servings.

Cereals

Most of us think of cereal as a bowl of Cheerios or Wheaties. Traditional cereals, however, are great and great for you. A hot bowl of mush was basic American frontier food not just for breakfast, but was served at almost every meal.

 Oatmeal

Oatmeal is the most consumed hot cereal in the country. Most of this is, unfortunately, the instant variety, which bears little resemblance in flavor and texture to a traditional, cooked version. The trick is to find the thickest oats you can. Old fashioned rolled oats are okay, but look out for #4 rolled oats—they are the best.

1/4 teaspoon salt
1 cup rolled oats or scotch oats
3 cups water (more for creamier oats, less for firmer)

There are two ways to make this.

You can do it all in one step. Bring water to boil in a saucepan. Stir in oats and salt. Cover and reduce heat to simmer slowly until water is absorbed, about 20 minutes. Remove from heat and let sit 5 minutes.

To save time in the morning, add the oats and salt to the boiling water the night before. Remove from heat and cover. In the morning, bring to a simmer over medium low heat for about 5 minutes.

Serve hot plain or with milk, sugar, honey, syrup, butter or whatever. At Allens Hill Farm, we love it with our signature Apple Cider Molasses, Apple or Apple Cinnamon Syrup.

Makes 4 servings.

Variations

- Add one-half cup raisins or dried fruit during cooking
- Add one chopped apple
- Add two tablespoons Allens Hill Farm Apple Cider Molasses

Cornmeal Mush

Cornmeal mush was the basis of the frontier diet in many areas of early America. Though it probably won't become a staple of your diet, it really should be tried if for no other reason than to gain an appreciation of what our ancestors did to survive.

4 cups water
1 cup cornmeal
1 teaspoon salt

Bring three cups of water and salt to the boil. Mix cornmeal with remaining cup of water. Pour this mix into boiling water in a thin stream stirring constantly. Continue stirring over medium heat for 8–10 minutes until thick. Serve hot with butter, milk, sugar, syrup, etc.

Makes 4 servings.

Fried Cornmeal Mush

This is pure frugal Americana. Take leftover cornmeal mush and put into a greased loaf pan. Cover and refrigerate. When firm, slice about one-half-inch thick. Dust with flour and fry in a pan with butter.

Serve warm with maple syrup or Allens Hill Farm Apple Syrup.

Granola

This is easy to make and good for you. Allens Hill Farm Apple Cider Molasses gives this a unique taste. If you prefer, use regular molasses or honey.

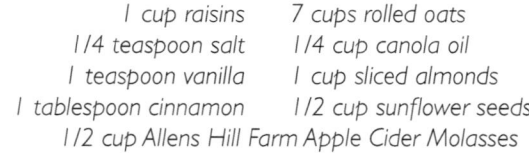

1 cup raisins *7 cups rolled oats*
1/4 teaspoon salt *1/4 cup canola oil*
1 teaspoon vanilla *1 cup sliced almonds*
1 tablespoon cinnamon *1/2 cup sunflower seeds*
1/2 cup Allens Hill Farm Apple Cider Molasses

Preheat the oven to 300°F. In a large mixing bowl combine all the dry ingredients except for the raisins. Stir in molasses, oil and vanilla until oats are well coated. Spread onto two baking sheets. Bake for 30 minutes, stirring after 15 minutes. Let cool. Stir in raisins. Store in an airtight container.

Makes about 2 quarts of cereal.

Eggs

Eggs in all shapes and forms are a quintessential breakfast food. They can be as simple as a fried or boiled egg, or elegant as in Eggs Benedict.

No matter how you choose to prepare them, they are fabulous in flavor and as versatile as your imagination. They are also a great source of protein at an economical cost.

If you have an opportunity, stop by your local farm market and buy some free-range eggs. There is a significant difference in flavor from store bought eggs. You may also notice the yolks have a more intense color.

Eggs should be one of the first foods you teach your kids to cook. They will learn a quick, nutritious dish as well as basic cooking skills and confidence with the stove.

To salt or not to salt?

Conventional wisdom is that salt toughens the egg when cooked. Science tells us, however, that salt interacts with the proteins in the egg to produce a more tender egg. This is also true of acidic ingredients. Milk and sugar will have a similar effect on eggs.

Boiled Eggs

Boiled eggs were likely one of the very first cooked foods.
How many other foods come in a disposable cooking container?

Hard Boiled Eggs

Simple hard-boiled eggs are great for breakfast, and can be included for lunch or a quick snack. Plus, they are a fine addition or garnish for many dishes.

Place eggs in a pan with cold water to cover. Bring to a boil and reduce heat to simmer to maintain a gentle boil for 10 minutes. If you prefer a firmer yolk, cook as long as 15 minutes. Serve hot or cool in a coldwater bath.

Soft Boiled Eggs

Follow the same procedure as for hard-boiled eggs. Cook for about 5 minutes, more or less, depending on how soft you like the yolks.

Poached Eggs

Poached eggs were quite common when I was growing up. Making poached eggs requires practice to develop a good technique, which prevents the white from dissipating into a cloud in the water.

Fill a pot or large saucepan about halfway with water. Add about a tablespoon of white vinegar for each quart of water (remember our science note about acid and eggs?). Heat to just below boil (200°F). Boiling water will cause the eggs to disintegrate. The freshest possible eggs work best. Crack each egg into a cup or saucer. Gently slide into the water. Cook 3–4 minutes. Remove from water with a skimmer and allow to drain. Serve as desired on toast, muffins, hash etc.

Fried Eggs

The only tricky part of cooking fried eggs is making sure the yolks remain intact. Two eggs per serving are standard. A good nonstick skillet makes the job a breeze; you shouldn't even need a spatula. If you like sunny side up with firm yolks have a lid handy.

Break the eggs into a small bowl. Heat the pan and add a tablespoon (or less depending on your preference and how well the pan is seasoned) of butter. When the butter stops foaming, slide in the eggs and immediately reduce heat to low. (Eggs can be easily overcooked. Low heat provides the best results). Cook until the whites have set and the yolks are cooked to desired doneness. If you want sunny side up with firmer yolks, cover pan. If you prefer over easy, gently flip and cook a few more seconds.

⇝ Scrambled Eggs ⇜

This is a required kid recipe. Everyone must know how to cook scrambled eggs!

A couple of basic do's and don'ts for scrambled eggs: Don't over-beat the eggs. A few good strokes with a whisk or fork are sufficient to break up the yolks. Too much force will make for eggs that are tough.

Cook over low heat. This will keep the eggs moist. The more slowly you cook your eggs the softer and more tender they will be. Don't overcook!

If you like to add ingredients to your eggs, that's fine. Salt and milk will also make the eggs more tender.

2 eggs
2 teaspoons butter
dash salt to taste
1–2 tablespoons milk to taste (optional)

Melt the butter in a skillet over low heat. Beat the eggs and add salt and milk if desired. Pour into skillet and stir constantly with a spatula or wooden spoon until just done (moist and tender).

Makes 1 serving.

Variations

⇝Scrambled eggs are a blank palate. You can add just about any cooked meat, vegetable or cheese.

Simply add the meat and or vegetables with the eggs. If you wish to add cheese, just sprinkle over the top when the eggs are done.

You can also sprinkle in some of your favorite chopped fresh herbs.

⇝ Omelets ⇜

Omelets are the "uptown" cousin of scrambled eggs. They differ in that they are cooked over high heat, stuffed and folded into an envelope.

There are innumerable variations on the basic omelet. Be creative and have fun.

There is no reason that once scrambled eggs have been mastered, kids can't learn the basic techniques of making an omelet.

2 or 3 eggs
salt to taste
1 tablespoon butter
1–2 tablespoons of milk or cream (optional)

Beat eggs and add salt and milk if desired. Heat a 7- or 8-inch skillet over high heat. Add butter and swirl in pan. When it stops foaming, pour in eggs. With a spatula, gently push coagulated eggs into center from the edge of pan until eggs are fully formed. Reduce heat.

Add fillings and seasonings. Let the eggs finish cooking. Loosen the omelet from the pan by running spatula along the edge and gently shaking the pan. Fold in half to cover the fillings. Slide onto plate and serve.

Makes 1 serving.

Fillings

- Almost any cooked meat or sausage is great in an omelet. Bacon is common, as is ham, but chicken or even seafood works well.

- Fresh herbs can make a wonderful omelet filling.

- Vegetables are an excellent addition. Mushrooms, peppers and onions are common. Asparagus is unbelievable. I prefer the vegetables to be cooked; the flavor and texture better complements the eggs

- Cheddar, Swiss or just about any cheese will work with an omelet. Try to pick a cheese that compliments the other fillings.

- Just about anything is fair game for an omelet. Throw caution to the wind. Express yourself and enjoy.

My Late Night Omelet

When I worked in restaurants and got home late and I wanted a quick, hot and flavorful meal with minimum effort, I would whip up one of these babies.

3 eggs
pepper to taste
oregano to taste
1 tablespoon butter
1 slice of provolone
3–4 slices hard salami, cut into quarters

Cook the salami in your pan over medium heat until it releases its oil. Set aside.

Increase heat to high and add butter. Cook omelet as above adding cooked salami, cheese and seasonings.

You can even top with warm marinara sauce if you are so inclined.

Makes 1 serving.

 Breakfast Sandwiches

There is no real trick to making a breakfast sandwich. Assemble them any way you like. Whether it's made on a muffin, biscuit or bagel, has eggs or not, a breakfast sandwich is always satisfying.

The "Bread"

You can use almost anything to enclose the fillings of a breakfast sandwich. Of course, the most common would be an English muffin, biscuit (see recipes on pages 131-133), or a bagel. There are many other options.

A nice sandwich roll is fine, as is a croissant. Use a flour tortilla or crepe. Make small pancakes or waffles. A couple of pieces of toast work fine, too.

The Eggs

Almost any type of egg will work in a breakfast sandwich. The trick is to make sure that the egg ends up being about the size of the bread you will be using. If it's too big for the bread, it can be a mess.

When making a fried egg, an egg ring can help control the size. If you don't have one, just keep the white under control by pushing it toward the yolk as it begins to set. Often, the yolk is broken and the egg if flipped to make sure the yolk is fully cooked.

If making scrambled eggs, I usually cook on high heat like an omelet, since it holds together better. You can certainly cook traditional scrambled eggs, but they will be messier and will fall out of the sandwich more easily.

The Meat

Bacon should be cooked crisp. You may want to cut the strips in half so they don't stick out too far from the bread.

Canadian bacon works well since the shape and size give perfect coverage over the whole sandwich.

If you like sausage, get bulk and form the patties like a thin hamburger. Sliced ham works well too.

Garnishes

Sliced or grated cheeses are the most common additions. However, salsa, hollandaise or cheese sauces are fun options.

Breakfast Sides

Side dishes can make the meal. What's better for breakfast than a few strips of crisp bacon or a steaming pile of home fries? Sides are also a way to make sure that breakfast is a balanced meal by adding fresh fruit or applesauce.

HOME FRIES

Home fries were the way my mother used up leftover boiled potatoes. You can easily make home fries fresh from raw potatoes as well. Either way, home fries can be a nice side dish to serve not only with breakfast items, but also with entrees at supper.

> 4 cooked or raw potatoes   salt and pepper to taste
> oil, shortening or bacon fat   1–2 cloves garlic (optional)
> 1 small onion

If using raw potatoes, clean and scrub. Do not peel. Cut into half-inch slices, then cut the slices into half-inch strips, then cut strips into half-inch cubes. Put into a pot and just cover with cold water. Add a teaspoon of salt. Place pot on the stove over high heat and bring to a boil. Cook 1 minute and drain.

If using cooked potatoes, cut into cubes as above.

Put a large skillet on the stove on medium high heat. When pan is hot, add oil, shortening or bacon fat. Bacon fat provides the best flavor. Add the potatoes and stir. Add salt and pepper.

While the potatoes are cooking, peel and chop the onion and garlic. Cook until the potatoes begin to turn a nice golden brown and add the onions and garlic. (Adding the onions too soon will cause them to burn before the potatoes are cooked).

If you are using leftover potatoes, they will cook quickly and they are more tender, so stir gently to avoid breaking them apart.

When the potatoes are golden brown and the onions clear, they are ready to serve.

Makes 4 servings.

Hash Browns

Hash browns are a bit different from home fries, since they are made from shredded potatoes. They are more like a potato pancake.

4 potatoes
1 small onion
salt and pepper to taste
vegetable oil, shortening or bacon fat

Wash and scrub the potatoes. Shred the potatoes. Using paper towels or a kitchen towel, press out as much moisture as possible; put potatoes into a mixing bowl. Peel and chop onion and mix into potatoes. Place a medium size non-stick skillet on the stove on medium high heat. When hot, add oil, fat or shortening. Put potatoes into skillet so they completely cover the bottom of the pan. Press down firmly. Sprinkle with salt and pepper. Cover pan and cook until the underside of the potatoes are a nice golden brown.

Remove the cover. Slide the hash browns onto a plate. Add a little more oil to the pan, then, using the plate, flip the hash browns back into the pan to cook the other side. When the bottom is golden brown, remove from pan and cut into wedges to serve.

Makes 4 servings.

Bacon

Most of us tend to eat bacon only occasionally. Therefore, I would recommend buying good quality, thick sliced bacon. To reduce shrinkage, start in a cold pan and don't cook with high heat.

Canadian Bacon

Canadian bacon is made from pork loin so it is much leaner than regular bacon. It cooks very quickly so be careful not to overcook or it will become tough.

Sausage

Sausage is a common breakfast meat. You can buy fresh or frozen patties or links, however, making your own breakfast sausage is simple. There is no comparison in the quality between store bought and homemade. Your sausage will be leaner, more flavorful, fresher and free of additives and preservatives.

If you have a meat grinder, buy pork butts. Trim the meat off the bones and as much fat as you like. If you don't have a meat grinder, just buy ground pork. Leave some fat, or the sausage will be too dry. This will make about five pounds, so freeze extra in bags or roll into logs and wrap tightly so you can just slice it into patties.

>
> 5 lbs. ground pork
> 2 tablespoons salt
> 1/2 teaspoon ginger
> 1-1/2 teaspoons nutmeg
> 1 cup ice water
> 1/4 teaspoon cayenne
> 1-1/2 teaspoons thyme
> 1 tablespoon rubbed sage
> 1-1/2 teaspoons ground white pepper

Keeping the meat as cold as possible, mix all the ingredients together with your hands. Freeze whatever you don't plan on cooking. Pat sausage into patties. Cook in a skillet on medium heat until well browned and an internal temperature of 165°F.

Makes about 5 pounds of sausage.

Yogurt Parfait

> yogurt
> Allens Hill Farm Granola
> Allens Hill Farm Let's Dukkah Breakfast
> Allens Hill Farm Apple Cinnamon Syrup

In a glass, alternately layer yogurt and the Allens Hill Farm Granola of your choice. Top the last layer of yogurt with Allens Hill Farm Apple Cinnamon Syrup or Allens Hill Farm Let's Dukkah Breakfast.

Allens Hill Farm Granola

Let's Do Lunch

You don't need a recipe to tell you how to make a sandwich. Wasn't a peanut butter and jelly sandwich one of your first culinary creations? Lunch is a great opportunity to "clean out the fridge." Leftovers from previous meals make great quick and easy lunches, especially if you plan it that way and make extra food to assure leftovers. If not, I'll give you a few fun lunch recipes.

Garbage Plate™

If you ever happen to be in Rochester, New York, and want a unique cultural and culinary experience, stop by Nick Tahou's on Main street for their one and only Garbage Plate™. It isn't elegant, but it's all good and all Rochester. A heaping plate of home fries and macaroni salad topped with two grilled Zwiegle hots covered with mustard, chopped onions and their signature meat sauce with a side of local Italian bread and butter.

I offer a reasonable facsimile. If you've been to Nick's for a plate, you know French fries are fine in place of home fries, baked beans instead of mac salad, and burgers instead of dogs. It's all good.

Sadly, Nick passed away a few years ago. He would always sit with my wife and me whenever we were there for lunch (more due to my wife's presence than mine). He always greeted us by pointing to my wife and saying "beauty" then to me "beast." Then he always told his favorite joke. "You know, my wife said when we first got married that she thought she was marrying a Greek god, instead she ended up with a God damned Greek!" Here's to you Nick!

mustard
meat sauce
8 Zwiegle hots
Italian bread with butter
1 large onion finely chopped
home fries (recipe on page 46)
3 pints plain macaroni salad (store bought is fine or make your own)

First, prepare the meat sauce. This can be done ahead of time.

dash nutmeg
1-1/4 cups water
1/2 teaspoon paprika
1/2 pound ground beef
1 tablespoon of minced onion
1/2 teaspoon salt
1/4 teaspoon thyme
1/4 teaspoon cayenne
1/2 teaspoon chili powder
1/2 teaspoon black pepper

In a small saucepan add all ingredients except water. Cook over medium heat until lightly browned. Reduce heat, add water, cover and simmer slowly for about 90 minutes. Remove cover and cook for about another 90 minutes until the liquid is reduced to the point where it just covers the meat. It will still be thin with pebbles of meat when spooned up.

To make the plate, first cook the hots. Preheat a large skillet or griddle to medium. Split the hots lengthwise taking care to not cut all the way through the one side so they open like a book. Lay flat on the griddle, cut side down first and cook until done, flipping halfway through. While the dogs are cooking, assemble the plates. Put a heaping mound of home fries on one side and macaroni salad on the other. Flatten slightly. Place 2 cooked hots, cut side up, on top, spread on mustard, sprinkle with a couple of tablespoons of chopped onion and the ladle a couple of tablespoons of hot sauce over everything. Serve with a couple of big slices of Italian bread and butter, with a bottle of ketchup and Tabasco sauce.

Makes 4 servings.

Patty Melt

I don't know about you, but the same old burger on a bun with fixin's can become a bit tiresome. I love patty melts: a burger topped with melted Swiss and grilled onions nestled between 2 slices of grilled rye bread. The following recipe is for 4 sandwiches.

1 large onion
salt and pepper
4 slices Swiss cheese
2 pounds ground beef
8 slices good quality seeded rye bread
2 tablespoons butter plus additional for spreading on bread

Divide ground beef into four parts and form into half-pound patties. Wrap and refrigerate. Peel and thinly slice onion. Melt butter in small sauté pan over medium low heat. Add onions and cook slowly until they are soft and begin to caramelize about 15 minutes or more. While onions are cooking, preheat large skillet or griddle. Unwrap burgers, season with salt and pepper and grill until done. While burgers are cooking prepare to assemble sandwiches. Place cooked burger on a slice of bread, top with slice of Swiss cheese, and cooked onions. Cover with second slice of bread and butter the outside. Clean griddle of meat juices and set to medium high heat. Place sandwich buttered side down. Butter the top slice. Grill until nicely golden brown, flip and cook until bottom is golden brown. Remove from grill, cut on a diagonal and serve on plate with chips or fries and a pickle.

Makes 4 servings.

❦ Ten Minute Pizza ❦

This is the ultimate kid friendly cooking experience. Kids love pizza and there is really no wrong way to make it. They can also immediately taste the results of the culinary choices.

Is there anyone who doesn't like pizza? You can satisfy your cravings with a quick lunch pizza. Just be sure to keep the basics on hand and any time can be "Pizza Time".

The crust: Just about anything will work. I prefer French or Italian bread. Cut a length proportional to your hunger, 6–8 inches is a good size, split open and you're in business. My son prefers English muffins. Bagels are fine. For a thin crust, flour tortillas are great.

The sauce: A jar of pizza sauce is a staple in our house; always ready to go. I also like to use olive oil instead.

The cheese: I buy five-pound blocks of mozzarella from my wholesale club; much more economical than the supermarket. Shred what you need. I always mix in some grated parmesan which keeps the mozzarella from clumping and adds a nice flavor and texture.

The toppings: use whatever you like or have on hand; pepperoni, ham, sausage, salami, peppers, onions, mushrooms. It's all good. My new favorite is fresh garlic which adds spice and flavor. You can also use leftover chicken, meatballs, etc.

Spices: to me a pizza is incomplete without a healthy dose of oregano. You can also spice it up with some red pepper flakes.

Preheat oven to 425°F. Put the bread of choice on a baking sheet. Spread on sauce, top with cheese, sprinkle on spices and load up the toppings. Pop into the oven for 5–15 minutes depending on what type of crust you use until cheese in melted.

Lovely Leftover Lunch

Just about any of the recipes in the supper section are excellent leftover for lunch candidates. This is where a microwave is a blessing. Zap for a few minutes and *voila*, a hot lunch. Some good choices are chili, stew, pasta, stir fry or soups. Leftover pot roast, chicken or meatloaf makes great sandwiches. There's nothing wrong with a cooked chicken leg or breast.

If you have chicken stock or broth, just put some into a bowl with leftover veggies, cooked pasta, cooked chicken and microwave. Instant soup!

The great cooks and chefs waste nothing. So if you are in the habit of pitching that little leftover bit of…., don't. That could be tomorrow's lunch. Besides, many dishes are even better the day after they are freshly prepared as flavors work their way through the food.

Most leftovers die of neglect. Too often they get put into a part of the fridge where they are hidden behind the more popular foods. Many times they are put into a container in which we can't see the contents or are not labeled. It's a good habit to go through the refrigerator at least once a week, preferably the day before trash day, and pitch what's bad and mentally inventory what needs to be used before it expires. Then use it up.

There's Nothing Wrong with Bringing Your Lunch

Have you ever done the math? If you are in the habit of eating out every day for lunch, add up what you spend in a week. A fast food meal is easily $5–$7. Want to get served? $10–$15. Toss in that morning coffee and you could be spending $50 or more each week. Ever wonder where those extra pounds come from? Think about the calories and fat consumed mindlessly at lunch.

Instead, make a sandwich. Pack a bag of carrot or celery sticks. Throw in an apple. Get a big bag of chips and throw a handful in a sandwich bag.

Try my math. A pound and a half of ham: $7. Loaf of bread: $1.50. Bag of chips: $2. Bag of carrots: $1.50. Bag of apples: $2. Total: $14. For the cost of one lunch out, you can eat better and healthier for a full week. Think about it.

This is a great lesson to impart to your kids as well. You can have some control over what they eat at school and they can take a part in their lunch choices. Teach them how to make a proper lunch and eventually, you won't have to be doing it for them. It's a great way to teach some independence and responsibility.

Patty Melt with Sweet Potato Chips
Recipes on pages 50 and 168

Supper

My father grew up on a farm. Dinner was the afternoon meal; the big meal of the day. Supper was what you ate after the day's work was done. Dinner was the main meal to replenish the body after morning chores and fuel up for the rest of the day. Supper was a lighter meal to be enjoyed after a long day of work. Bedtime came early, so a big meal at night wasn't desirable.

In our house the evening meal was "supper". Our suppers were the predictable standards of the 50's and 60's. It was fairly frugal fare: basic meat and potatoes. Casseroles were a mainstay as were many of the post war culinary classics such as stuffed peppers with Spanish rice, Beefaroni, macaroni and cheese, even the occasional Spam. You baby boomers know these well.

We also were expected to consume some of the foods that were part of the heritage of our parent's youth. I'm sure some of you remember, all too vividly, liver with bacon and onions. My wife's family had a tradition of eating scrapple. These foods do have their place, if for nothing else, than to remind us of the wonderful choices we have today.

In today's world the evening meal is, in many homes, an endangered species. Busy schedules and non-traditional jobs make a nightly sit down meal an increasingly difficult feat. Therefore, most of the recipes in this chapter are designed to be easy to prepare and quick to cook.

They are also meant to be economical. Many of these meals can be prepared for under $2.00 per portion; less than half of the cost of a meal at a fast food restaurant.

This chapter on supper is an homage to my father. (And Robert Duvall.... pay attention to how many times he refers to "supper" in his movies).

Establishing a Tradition

One of the best ways to make a meal special is to establish some rituals or traditions. When I was growing up I remember the Prince Spaghetti commercials. "Wednesday night is Prince Spaghetti night." In our house, Friday night is "Pizza Night." Every week the kids (and parents) look forward to homemade pizza.

Pick a night and a meal and make it fun.

Grilled Steak
Recipe on page 84

 # Quick One-Pan Dishes

These dishes are designed to be both simple to prepare and quick to clean up. One-pan meals also are full of flavor since nothing is lost in the cooking process. Though most are fairly complete, I'll offer some suggestions for accompaniments to round out the meal.

Note: Some recipes will use store-bought components to save time. Sometimes it's ok to cheat a little when you want to whip up a good meal fast.

⇾ Skillet Pasta ⇽

I rarely have time to make spaghetti and meatballs from scratch. However, I couldn't bring myself to use store bought skillet dinners. Instead, I just came up with my own. If you like a garden style sauce, add the optional vegetables.

This recipe is an opportunity for a young cook to gain confidence on the stovetop with a simple task of browning. Once that is accomplished, the rest of the recipe involves simply adding ingredients and an occasional stir. This is a perfect dish for a new cook to master.

3 cups hot water (approx.)
grated parmesan cheese (optional)
24 oz. jar red pasta sauce
2 cups pasta (I like penne or ziti)
red pepper flakes, basil, oregano, thyme (optional)
sliced mushroom, diced peppers and onions (optional)
1 pound ground beef, or Italian sausage, or other ground meat,
(you can use meatballs—recipe on following page) or a combination of these

You will need a large skillet for this dish. Place the pan over medium high heat. Add the ground meat, sausage, or meatballs and brown. If you are not using a non-stick pan, add a tablespoon or two of oil to prevent sticking. Stir until meat is cooked through. If you are adding the vegetables, toss them in now. Drain any excess fat that has accumulated in the pan during cooking. It isn't necessary to get every drop; there's a lot of flavor there.

Reduce heat to medium and add the pasta sauce. Stir well to deglaze the pan. The little bits of meat stuck to the pan add lots of flavor. Dump in the pasta and the water. Stir well. Stir occasionally until it just begins to bubble and reduce the heat to low; you want a slow simmer. Add optional seasonings and cheese if desired. Cook about 30 minutes or so, stirring occasionally, until pasta is cooked to your preference. Cooking time will vary depending on the type of pasta you use and the type of sauce. If the pasta is not cooking and the sauce seems very thick, add a bit more hot water.

Serve with good Italian bread or our favorite garlic bread (see recipe on page 108). Add a tossed salad to make an excellent meal.

Makes 6 servings.

Meatballs

There are as many meatball recipes as there are Italians. I typically vary my ingredients based on my mood or in what dish I'm using them. It's a great recipe to exercise your creativity. If you are unsure of your seasoning, fry a small bit until done and taste. Then correct your seasoning.

Put the "youngins" to work here. Place all of the ingredients in a bowl and let them get their hands into it (make sure they wash their hands thoroughly first). After it is mixed, they can form the meatballs. Have them use a ping pong ball or golf ball as a guide.

1 egg
salt and pepper to taste
2 tablespoons finely minced onion (optional)
1 tablespoon parsley (again fresh is better)
1 pound ground beef (or a mix of beef, pork and veal)
1/4 cup grated parmesan cheese (freshly grated if possible)
1–3 cloves minced garlic (depending on your love of garlic)
1/4 -1/2 teaspoons each oregano, basil and thyme, if desired, to taste
1 cup bread crumbs (approx.—I prefer plain so I can season them myself)

Put all ingredients into a mixing bowl. Mix until combined (hands are best here). Don't over-mix. Form into balls of desired size. Sautée in a pan over medium high heat with olive oil, turning often until nicely browned outside.

Makes 15 to 20 meatballs.

RED NECK STIR FRY
OR SMOKED SAUSAGE SKILLET DINNER

This is really a meal in itself, though a good loaf of crusty bread with butter or warm biscuits is a great addition.

This is a good dish to work on basic knife skills, since the whole recipe centers around cutting up vegetables and meat into chunks. Demonstrate how to properly hold a knife and the food while cutting. Discuss cross contamination issues, i.e. cutting vegetables before meat. Make sure the knife is sharp; remember fewer accidents occur with a sharp knife than a dull one. Also review what to do if you cut yourself.

1 large onion
2 cloves garlic
salt and pepper to taste
vegetable oil (or bacon fat)
1 large green or red bell pepper
1 pound or so of smoked sausage
half-dozen or so large white mushrooms
3 russet potatoes (other varieties are fine)
thyme and or rosemary to taste (optional)

Scrub the potatoes under running water to clean. Pat them dry with a paper towel. Cut the spuds into one-inch chunks and place on a microwavable plate. Put into the microwave about 10 minutes or so until they just begin to soften. (You can also accomplish this by putting the potatoes into a pot of water. Bring to the boil for just a minute and drain.)

While the potatoes are doing their thing, cut up the remaining vegetables and sausage into one-inch pieces. Also, peel and mince the garlic.

Put a large skillet on the stove. When hot, add enough oil to cover the bottom about one-eighth inch deep. (Bacon fat works well here. It adds great flavor, but may not be the best choice if you have health issues). Add the potatoes and cook, stirring frequently, until golden brown. Add more oil if needed. Remove the potatoes and set aside.

Add the cut up vegetables, garlic and sausage and cook, stirring frequently until the sausage is cooked and the vegetabes are just tender. Add the potatoes back in and stir. Add salt and pepper to taste and additional herbs if desired.

Makes 4 servings.

⁓ BONELESS CHICKEN AND RICE ⁓

You can do this a couple of ways: you can either make the rice from scratch or use a store-bought chicken rice mix.

2–3 boneless chicken breasts
chicken rice side dish mix prepared per directions
Or
1 cup rice
2 cups chicken stock

Cut the chicken breast into three-quarter-inch chunks. Sautee in a skillet with a little bit of oil or butter until just cooked. Remove from pan. If using a store-bought chicken rice mix, prepare per directions. Add chicken back to pan and cook per package directions.

If you use regular rice, when you remove the chicken, add a couple of tablespoons of butter or oil to the pan, add the rice and cook over medium heat for a couple of minutes. Add the chicken stock and the chicken and cook 15 – 20 minutes or until the liquid is absorbed. This goes well with steamed broccoli.

Makes 4 servings.

⁓ FRIED RICE ⁓

This is a great dish to get rid of leftovers kicking around in the fridge. Leftover pork, chicken, vegetables and rice are all you need to whip up a tasty meal. If you don't have leftovers, then use fresh. You can just cook up a chicken breast and cut into quarter-inch dice. Frozen or canned mixed vegetables work equally well. Either way, fried rice is a quick meal that's a great change of pace. This is also a dish where exact measurements don't matter at all.

Tip. To make fried rice, the rice you use must be pre-cooked and chilled.

pepper to taste
2 eggs, well beaten
1 cup mixed vegetables
2 tablespoons soy sauce
2 tablespoons vegetable oil
3–4 cups cooked cold rice
1-1/2 cups cooked cold chicken, pork or shrimp

Heat a large skillet or wok on high heat. When hot, add oil and rice. Stir frequently and cook until rice grains are separated. Add cooked meat, poultry or seafood and vegetables and continue to cook stirring frequently until they are heated through. Reduce heat and push rice mixture to one side. Using the beaten eggs, make scrambled eggs in the other side and break into small pieces. Stir the egg into the rice mixture. Stir in the soy sauce and add a dash of pepper if desired.

Makes 4 to 6 servings.

Super Simple Soup

This is another great way to work out leftovers. This works equally well with beef. You can easily double this and freeze what's left for a future meal.

There are many options for chicken stock; canned, frozen, homemade or from a base. Please don't use bullion cubes. I like using soup base. You can find it in most wholesale clubs. It's what restaurants use for soups, sauces and gravies. It's very economical (pennies per pint), has excellent flavor and it is virtually fat free. Just mix with water per the directions and you're in business.

The vegetables may either be raw, frozen, or leftover. Big pieces or small depending on you preference are equally acceptable.

I like to add a starch item as well. You can use noodles, pasta, rice or barley.

parsley
salt and pepper to taste
1 gallon chicken or beef stock
2 cups cooked chicken or beef
Assorted vegetables (carrots, onions, celery, etc.)
1 cup uncooked noodles, pasta, rice or barley (leftover cooked rice is fine, too)

If you do not have cooked chicken, you may use a couple of boneless breasts. Cook in a bit of oil in your soup pot to begin, and cut them up before adding the rest of the ingredients. I would not recommend doing this with the beef as it would be too tough if cooked this way.

In a stock pot, either add the prepared stock, or mix up the base and water per package directions. Add the vegetables, meat and parsley. Simmer until vegetables begin to become tender. Add noodles, rice, etc and cook until done.

Serve with a loaf of fresh crusty bread and a tossed salad.

Makes 8 servings.

Quick Beef Stew

This is the country cousin of the quick beef soup recipe above. If you have a leftover roast beef or steak and some vegetables, you're set.

1 quart beef stock
1/2 teaspoon thyme
2 tablespoons cornstarch
salt and pepper to taste
1/4 cup red wine (optional)
1 tablespoon Worcestershire sauce
6 large white mushrooms, quartered
2 cups leftover beef cut into one-inch cubes
1 cup each potatoes, peeled onions, peeled carrots, cut into one-inch chunks

Put stock into pot and bring to a boil. Add potatoes, carrots and onions and cook until the potatoes can just be pierced with a fork.

Mix cornstarch with one-quarter cup of water and stir into stew. Reduce to simmer and add beef, mushrooms, and seasonings. Do not let boil, it will toughen the beef.

Let cook at least 20 minutes. Longer is better. If it is not thick enough for you, add more cornstarch and water.

Serve with fresh bread or rolls to sop up the gravy.

Makes 6 servings.

Stir Fry

The key to a good stir fry is an interesting assortment of vegetables. As different choices become available throughout the growing season, use your creativity to keep your stir fries different and interesting.

I also like to avoid too many of the commercial oyster sauces, etc. I prefer to keep it light and simple. Soy sauce and sesame oil are excellent ingredients to keep on hand.

You can do this vegetarian if you like, but typically there would be a protein component. Just about anything works. Beef, chicken and pork are all good choices. You can even splurge with shrimp or other shellfish.

A wok is not necessary, but it does make things easier. If you don't own a wok, use the biggest skillet you have.

12 oz. raw beef, chicken or pork (approx.)

Stir Fry Marinade

salt and pepper 1 tablespoon vinegar
2 cloves garlic, minced 1 teaspoon sesame oil
2 tablespoons soy sauce 1 tablespoon sherry (optional)

Slice the beef, chicken or pork into thin (one-eighth inch) slices. Place in a small bowl and add remaining ingredients. Stir and refrigerate. Marinate for at least 15 minutes.

vegetable oil 2–3 peeled carrots
6 large mushrooms 1 large green pepper
1 large onion, peeled
Optional vegetables—zucchini, summer squash, cabbage, bok choi, etc.

Cut up your vegetables into one-inch pieces. Heat your wok on high heat. When very hot, add a couple of tablespoons of oil. Add vegetables and stir frequently until they are heated through. They should still be firm. Cook in multiple batches if necessary to avoid the pan from cooling too much. Put vegetables aside and bring pan back up to temperature. Add some more oil and add meat. Stir rapidly until cooked. Add cooked vegetables back to pan and stir to combine.

Serve with cooked rice.

Makes 4 servings.

Dukkah Fish
Recipe on page 82

 # Slow Cooking

These are foods that rely on slow, long cooking to develop flavor. Start these early and then get on with the rest of your day.

Slow-cooked meals also make great leftovers, so don't be afraid to make a double batch. You'll also find these foods taste better the next day as the flavors come together in the fridge.

A great way to have a wonderful supper is to take advantage of opportunities on days off to cook big batches and freeze meals for future use. Stews and chilis are perfect for this.

I'm not a crock pot person, but if you are, many of these recipes are certainly adaptable to that form of cooking. Refer to your instruction manual for tips on how to use these in your crock pot.

STEW

Stew is one of the first cooked foods. The concept is pretty simple, brown meat, add liquid and vegetables and cook until done.

The recipe below uses beef, but you can certainly use a different type of meat if you prefer. Veal and lamb are good choices. If you have access to specialty meats, try buffalo. Game can also be used; lots of hunters make venison stew. Simply adjust the type of herbs and seasonings based on the meat you use. The concepts are the same.

1 bay leaf
salt and pepper
8 large white mushrooms
oil, shortening or bacon fat
1 quart water (or beef stock)
1/2 cup flour
1 teaspoon thyme
1 large onion (or 12 baby)
other root vegetables (optional)
3–4 peeled carrots (or 8 oz. baby)
4 potatoes (or 1 pound small potatoes)
2 pounds stew beef cut into one-inch cubes

Prepare your vegetables. If using a large onion, peel and cut into one-inch chunks; just peel the baby onions. You may also use frozen baby onions. Peel and cut the carrots into thick slices or use peeled baby carrots. Wash and peel the potatoes (I prefer to leave the skins on). Cut into one-inch chunks. Or if you have small spuds just wash. If you like other root vegetables like turnip, rutabaga, etc, feel free to add what you like. Mushrooms should be washed and quartered. Peel and roughly chop garlic.

Mix flour, salt and pepper together on a large plate or piece of waxed paper. Put large pot or Dutch oven (I love to use my cast iron one) on high heat. Add oil, shortening or bacon fat to coat the bottom. Add onions and cook until golden brown. Just before onions are done, add the garlic and cook for a minute. Remove from pan.

Dust several cubes of meat and brown in pan. Don't put in too many at a time or the pieces will not brown. You want a nice caramelized crust for the best flavor. Continue to coat beef and brown until all are cooked. Add additional oil if needed. Bring water or stock to a boil in separate pot.

When the last batch is finished, reduce heat to medium and return all meat to pot. Pour in water or stock being careful to avoid splattering which may result. Stir the bottom of the pan to deglaze. Add bay leaf and reduce heat to simmer. Cover the pot and cook slowly for at least 2 hours until it becomes tender. Don't boil; it will make the meat tough.

Add potatoes, and carrots (add optional vegetables) and cook until carrots can just be pierced with a fork. Add onions, garlic and mushrooms and continue to cook until vegetables are cooked through. Taste and add salt and pepper to taste.

Serve with fresh bread or rolls.

Makes 6 servings.

Chili

Chili comes in all styles and flavors depending on what part of the country you are from. The fact that there are innumerable chili recipes is evidenced by the various chili contests which are held in almost every town in the country.

We'll keep our chili versions pretty basic, but feel free to be as creative as you want.

Chili Con Carne

This is the basic, standard chili made with ground beef and kidney beans. Of course if you aren't into beans, they can be omitted. However, the beans add a lot of nutritional value, texture and flavor. If you usually use canned beans, try dried beans instead. They have a much better texture and flavor.

If you want to perk up your chili, try using various dried chilies. We were raised on commercial chili powder. Ancho, Serrano, chipolte and other chilies can be toasted and ground into powder to give excellent flavor to your favorite chili.

1 large onion
2 cloves garlic
dash Tabasco sauce
1 pound ground beef
2 tablespoons vegetable oil
1 teaspoon cumin (optional)
1 pound dried kidney beans* or
1 large can (28 oz.) tomatoes (crushed)
1 large can (28 oz.) can kidney beans
2 tablespoons (or more to taste) chili powder

Peel and chop onion and garlic. If not using diced or crushed tomatoes, blend in a food processor or crush with your hands. Heat a large pot over medium high heat. When hot, add oil, ground beef, onions, garlic and chili powder. Cook, stirring often, until onion become translucent and beef is cooked. Drain any excess fat. Add tomatoes, beans and spices. Simmer slowly for a couple of hours or more.

Serve with cornbread (recipe on page 46). Garnish with cheese, sour cream and crackers.

Makes 6 servings.

*To cook dried beans, the traditional method is to soak overnight, drain, add fresh water and simmer until tender. There is really no need to soak. Rinse the beans. Add about 3 times the volume of water to beans and simmer slowly until done, at least an hour. When tender, drain beans.

Variations

Turkey Chili: simply substitute ground turkey for ground beef and don't use the bacon fat for a healthier version.

"Leftover" Chili: chili can also be another of those great ways to use of all kinds of leftover meats in the fridge. Instead of using ground beef, you can use up cooked pork, beef, chicken, turkey, hamburger and lamb. Simply substitute these for the ground beef in the Chili con carne recipe above.

Southwest Chili

Many purists insist that real chili is made with chunks of stew beef and no tomato sauce. It's more like the chuck wagon food in the old western movies. Beans are optional, but why forgo the "Blazing Saddles" effect?

1/4 cup flour
Tabasco to taste
1/4 teaspoon cumin
4 oz. dried ancho chilies
salt and pepper to taste
1 teaspoon dried oregano
Vegetable oil, shortening, or bacon fat
4 cloves garlic, peeled and minced
2 pounds stew beef or chuck steak, cut into one-inch cubes
1 pound dried kidney beans (optional–see recipe above for cooking instructions)

Make chili powder from the ancho chilies. It is wise to wear plastic gloves while handling chilies. Put a heavy skillet or griddle over medium heat. Take each chili, split and remove seeds. Put chilies on griddle and toast for a few seconds on each side until you hear them crackle. When done, put into a food processor (or keep a coffee grinder just for spices) and blend into a powder.

Heat a pot or Dutch oven over medium high heat. This is similar to making stew. When the pan is hot, coat the bottom with oil or shortening and brown cubes of beef in the pot. Continue to cook in batches until all beef is cooked. Add a bit of oil and cook the garlic for a minute or two.

Return the meat to the pot. Add the chili powder, flour and the rest of the herbs. Stir well. Add enough water to just cover the meat. Cover and reduce heat to simmer; do not boil or the meat will toughen. After an hour or so, add the beans and continue to cook until meat and beans are tender.

Serve with biscuits or cornbread.

Makes 4 to 6 servings.

Cincinnati Chili

When I was working in a restaurant, one of my prep cooks turned me on to this. She would bring it in for lunch and feed the whole kitchen crew. The combination of spices is unique and unusual. It is a Cincinnati trademark. This recipe will feed a bunch and can also be lots of fun at a tailgater.

The way Cincinnati chili is served is quite unique. Call it a progressive dish. "One way" is just the chili below. "Two way" is served over spaghetti. "Three way" is then garnished with shredded cheddar cheese. "Four way" means you top that with chopped onions. Finally, "Five way", the *pièce de résistance*, the whole shebang, is topped with kidney beans!

      2 bay leaves 1/4 cup vinegar
     2 teaspoons cumin 1 teaspoon paprika
    2 teaspoons allspice 1/4 cup chili powder
    2 teaspoons oregano 1/2 teaspoon nutmeg
    2 pounds ground beef salt and pepper to taste
    2 teaspoons cinnamon 1 pound cooked spaghetti
  2 tablespoons vegetable oil 1-28 oz. can tomatoes, blended
1 large onion, peeled and chopped 2 tablespoons Worcestershire sauce
1/4 cup unsweetened cocoa powder 1 teaspoon Tabasco (or more to taste)
    4 cloves garlic, peeled and chopped

  Heat a large stockpot over medium high heat. Add oil, ground beef, onions, garlic and chili powder. Cook until beef is cooked and onions become translucent. Stir frequently; you want the ground beef to be completely broken up. Add remaining ingredients and simmer for 1–2 hours. If it looks a bit dry, add additional water. It should resemble a pebbly, rather thin, sauce when done.

Garnishes
1 cup chopped onions
2 cups shredded cheddar cheese
1 pound cooked kidney beans (see recipe above)

  Serve over the hot spaghetti and let everyone add the garnish they like. I like this with good Italian bread on the side. A cold beer isn't bad either.

  Makes 6 to 10 servings (depending on if you serve with beans and spaghetti).

 JAMBALAYA

This is a great cold day, stick-to-your-ribs meal: hot, filling and a bit spicy.

       1 bay leaf 1/4 cup olive oil
      1 cup diced ham 1 teaspoon thyme
     4 cups chicken stock 1 tablespoon parsley
     2 cups uncooked rice salt and pepper to taste
    4 stalks celery, chopped 1/8 teaspoon cayenne pepper
    1 green pepper, chopped 2 medium tomatoes, chopped
 1 large onion, peeled and chopped 1 whole chicken cut into pieces
2 garlic cloves, peeled and chopped 1/2 pound cooked smoked sausage

Preheat the oven to 325°F. Heat a large skillet on medium high heat. Pat chicken pieces dry with a paper towel. Add olive oil to hot pan. Place in chicken pieces, skin side down. (Be careful of splatters). When the first side is nicely browned, turn over. Sprinkle with salt, fresh ground pepper and cayenne. When the chicken is done, remove from pan and set aside. Note: you can either remove the chicken from the bones, or leave the pieces intact.

Add the peppers, onion, garlic, celery, sausage and ham to the pan and cook until vegetables are tender. Add the tomatoes and cook until they release their moisture. Add the rice and stir to coat the grains. Add the chicken broth, and herbs. If you picked the chicken from the bones add now. Stir and dump into a large baking dish. If you left the chicken pieces whole, lay on top of the mixture.

Cover and bake for about an hour or until rice is cooked and liquid is absorbed. If the Jambalaya seems to be drying out, add additional water of chicken stock.

Makes 6 servings.

~ Sausage, Peppers and Onions ~

This is so simple and so good. I learned this from our next door neighbors, the DiLella's, when I was a kid. It was a staple dish at almost any family or neighborhood gathering. Be sure to buy some good sausage rolls or Italian bread to serve these in. You can scale this recipe up as much as needed depending on the size of your crowd.

This is a recipe that young cooks can do start to finish. All they need are some basic knife skills. Wouldn't it be nice to have your kids make you dinner for a change?

salt to taste
4 sausage or sub rolls
1 clove garlic, peeled and minced
1 large green pepper cut into half-inch strips
1 large onion, peeled and cut into half-inch slices
1 pound sweet or hot Italian sausage cut into four pieces

Preheat oven to 325°F. Spray a baking dish with non-stick cooking spray. Lay sausage on the bottom. Strew onions, peppers, garlic over the top. Sprinkle with salt to taste. Cover pan and put into oven. Bake 30–40 minutes or until sausage reaches a minimum internal temp of 165°F. Serve in rolls.

Makes 4 servings.

Variation

On the stovetop: this can be prepared in a skillet as well. It is quicker from start to finish, but does require more attention as you need to turn the sausage and stir the peppers and onions to ensure even cooking. Simply add a little olive oil to a large skillet on medium heat and add the remaining ingredients. Cook until the sausages are nicely browned and reach a minimum internal temperature of 165°F, about 15–20 minutes. The vegetables should be just tender.

Pot Roast

A great pot roast relies on very slow cooking to produce a fall apart tender roast and rich flavor. A cast iron Dutch oven is perfect for this dish. Success also depends on choosing a cut of meat that is not too lean. A nice thick chuck roast is my favorite.

3 potatoes	1/4 cup flour
1 teaspoon thyme	salt and pepper to taste
6 large white mushrooms	2 cups water or beef stock
1-1/2-inch thick chuck roast	3 carrots or 8 oz. baby carrots
About 1/4 cup oil or shortening	1 clove of garlic, peeled and minced

Heat the Dutch oven over medium high heat. On a plate or piece of wax paper, mix flour with salt and pepper. Coat the outside of the roast with the flour mixture. Add oil or shortening to coat the bottom of the pan. Put the roast into the pan and brown on both sides. Add garlic and cook for a minute more. Reduce heat and add water or stock, bay leaf and thyme. Cover and let cook until beef is tender, 3–4 hours. Make sure the liquid does not come to a boil, or the meat will toughen.

About an hour before serving, prepare the vegetables. Wash the potatoes and cut into one-inch chunks. Peel and thickly slice the carrots. Wash and quarter the mushrooms. Add to the pot roast and continue to cook until the potatoes are tender.

Before serving, remove the roast and let rest for 10 minutes or so before carving. If you wish to serve gravy, remove the vegetables and set aside to keep warm. Put the pan on the stove and bring the juices to a boil. While it is heating up, mix two tablespoons of cornstarch with two tablespoons of water. Stir this into the boiling juice to thicken, and then reduce heat.

Carve the meat and place on a platter. Arrange the vegetables around the beef. Serve the gravy on the side.

Makes 4 servings.

Casseroles

Casseroles were a mainstay of 50's and 60's fare. Many are probably best left as a memory. Who can forget (as hard as we may try) tuna noodle and pea casserole or the hot dog casserole with cornbread over the top?

Still, there are a few that are worth adding to our repertoire.

Ed's Favorite Mac and Cheese

When I was in college, it quickly became apparent to my apartment mates that my culinary skills were too good to waste. So in exchange for cooking dinner, I was exempt from the remaining group chores. This dish was a favorite, especially with my roommate, Ed. When he comes to visit, I still make it a point to whip up a batch of his favorite macaroni and cheese.

I think the key to this dish is to find the best extra sharp cheddar you can find. However, if your kids are used to mac&cheese out of a box, use half Velveeta and half sharp cheddar. Also feel free to use your favorite pasta shape if you don't like the traditional elbows.

Knowing how to make a basic white sauce is a great skill to acquire. It's also an opportunity to teach kids what real macaroni and cheese is compared to that atrocious stuff out of a cardboard box. Let them shred the cheese and learn how to cook pasta to al dente.

1 cup milk
salt and pepper
cayenne pepper
2 tablespoons flour
2 tablespoons butter
1-1/2 cups elbow macaroni
1-1/2 cups shredded cheddar cheese

Preheat oven to 350°F. Spray a casserole dish with non-stick cooking spray. Shred cheddar cheese and set aside. Cook macaroni in a pot of salted water until al dente and drain completely in a colander. While pasta is cooking, melt butter in a saucepan. Add flour and stir to combine. Cook over medium heat for about 2 minutes; do not let brown. Slowly add milk and whisk with a wire whip of fork making sure to eliminate any lumps. When all milk is added, continue to stir until sauce thickens. Remove from the heat and add a dash of cayenne and stir in shredded cheese. Stir cheese sauce into cooked pasta and then pour into prepared casserole. Smooth the top.

Bake in oven 30–40 minutes until it is bubbly and a nice brown on top. Serve with green beans or a tossed salad.

Makes 4 to 6 servings.

Baked Ziti

This is quick and easy to make. Be sure to have a nice salad and loaf of Italian bread or garlic bread to serve along side.

2 cups uncooked ziti
1-24 oz. jar pasta sauce
grated Parmesan cheese
1/2 pound shredded mozzarella cheese
1 pound ground beef, Italian sausage or meatballs

Preheat oven to 350°F. Spray a baking dish with non-stick cooking spray. Shred the cheese and add a couple of tablespoons of grated parmesan and mix. The parmesan adds flavor, texture and keeps the mozzarella from clumping. Cook the ziti in boiling salted water until al dente. Drain and set aside.

Cook your chosen meat in a skillet, or go meatless. When done, add pasta sauce to heat. Dump into bowl of cooked pasta and mix well. Dump into prepared baking dish and sprinkle shredded cheese over top. I like to sprinkle oregano over the top as well.

Bake in oven 20 minutes or until bubbly and cheese is melted. Serve with garlic bread and a tossed salad.

Makes 6 servings.

Scalloped Potatoes and Ham

This is a great way to use up leftover ham; a good stick-to-your-ribs meal.

The recipe is really just a guide. Just keep repeating the steps until you either use up your ingredients or your baking dish is full.

1 stick butter
milk as needed
fresh ground pepper to taste
1-12 oz. can evaporated milk
1/2 cup flour or more as needed
2 cups cooked ham in bite-sized pieces
4 potatoes, washed and thinly sliced (peel if you like)

Preheat oven to 350°F.

Spray a casserole dish with non-stick cooking spray.

All you have to do is layer the casserole as follows until full. Start with a layer of potato slices on the bottom. Be sure to overlap them slightly. Next add some of the ham pieces. Sprinkle lightly with flour and add a few pats of butter. Grind some pepper over the top if you desire. Repeat this layering, pressing gently down on the potato layer each time, until the casserole is full, ending on a potato layer.

Pour the evaporated milk over the top of the potatoes until the level of the milk is about one-quarter inch below the top level of the potatoes.

Cover the casserole and bake for about an hour or until the potatoes are tender.

Remove the cover about halfway through to allow the top to brown. If it browns too quickly, simply replace the cover.

Makes 4 to 6 servings.

Variation

Twice-Baked Potatoes and Ham: this is our new favorite way to use up leftover ham. Simply follow the recipe for Twice-Baked Potatoes on page 105 and omit the bacon. Add two cups of ham and bake as directed.

 # Meats

The following section is devoted to some of the common meat dishes you would normally prepare for supper. They are quick, easy to make and economical.

Pork Chops

Pork chops are one of the simplest and quickest main dishes to prepare. There are several different types of chops, most commonly rib and center cut. I prefer to cut my own by buying whole pork loins at a local wholesale club. You can't beat the price. Cut them as thick or thin as you like, or leave yourself a roast. You end up with boneless chops which have almost no extra fat. Plus, you can portion into bags that give you the precise number of portions you need, eliminating waste.

I like to serve fresh apple sauce with pork chops. Mashed potatoes and a hot vegetable make an admirable meal. If you are a sauerkraut fan, by all means put some out with your chops.

Pan Fried Pork Chops

Pork chops will stay tender if they are cooked at a lower temperature. I start them in a cold pan.

4 pork chops
1 tablespoon butter
*Grill Seasoning (see **Pantry Checklist** on page 175)*

It doesn't get any easier than this. Lightly sprinkle grill seasoning on one side of the chops. Put the chops in the pan, seasoned side down. Place the pan on the stove on medium heat. When you see moisture begins to form on the top of the chop, season the top side. Add butter to the pan. When it has melted, flip the chops. Continue to cook until they reach an internal temperature of 165°F. The flesh will become pale and the juices from the chop should be clear. Cooking time will vary based on thickness of the chops.

You can make a quick sauce for the chops simply by deglazing the pan. Remove the chops and return the pan to the heat. Increase to high. Add about one-quarter cup of water and bring to a boil. Scrape the bottom of the pan with a spatula to deglaze. You can even add a dollop of butter to add richness. Pour juice over chops.

Makes 4 servings.

Glazes

You can perk up chops simply by brushing on a glaze when done. Allens Hill Farm Spiced Apple Glaze or Smokey Apple Glaze is perfect for chops. Simply brush some glaze onto the chop a minute or so before you remove from the pan. Allens Hill Farm Apple Cider Molasses also makes a great glaze.

Breaded Pork Chops

A great American company made a fortune by simply putting some breading and seasoning in a bag and getting us to toss our chops in the bag and shake it. Trust me: you can do the same yourself for just pennies. Besides, you can season your own breading to suit your taste.

There are two options here. The "shake in the bag" technique is quicker and less messy, but will not result in as thick and consistent a layer of breading. The more traditional method of dipping in egg wash before breading produces a better breaded product. This basic technique can be applied to many types of meat, poultry and seafood by simply adjusting the seasonings.

4 pork chops

For breading:
1 teaspoon sage
1/4 teaspoon thyme
salt and pepper to taste
1 teaspoon parsley flakes
1/4 teaspoon granulated garlic
2 cups bread crumbs

For egg wash
1 egg
1/2 cup flour
1/2 cup milk

Preheat the oven to 375°F. Mix breadcrumbs with seasonings. If you are using the "shake" method, put into a gallon plastic bag. If you are using the more traditional method, place into shallow bowl.

Shake method: this is great kid fun. Rinse chops in water. Place into bag one at a time. Close bag and shake to coat chop. Remove chop from bag and put on sheet pan. When all chops are coated, place in oven and bake 20–30 minutes or until they reach an internal temperature of 165°F. The cooking time will vary with the thickness of the chop.

Traditional method: this is great messy kid fun. Be sure to show them the "wet hand/dry hand" technique: using one hand for dipping in the egg wash and the other for breading the chop. This prevents them from breading their fingers.)

You need three dishes for this method. For the first step, use a small plate to contain the flour. The second should be a small bowl in which you beat the egg and then beat in the milk to make the egg wash. The third will be the shallow bowl containing your breading. Pat the chops dry with a paper towel. One at a time, dust the chops in flour. Then dip into the second bowl and coat with egg wash. Remove and place into the breading and coat completely.

Remove chop from bowl and put on the sheet pan. When all chops are coated, place in oven and bake 20–30 minutes or until they reach an internal temperature of 165°F. The cooking time will vary with the thickness of the chop.

Makes 4 servings.

Baked Pork Chops with Stuffing

This is a recipe where I admit I cheat. I use a store bought stuffing mix. It's very quick and makes a nice change of pace. If you are more of a purist, see the Stuffing recipe on page 108.

4 pork chops
salt and pepper
1 apple, peeled and sliced (optional)
1 package stuffing mix, prepared per directions
Allens Hill Farm Smoked Apple or Spiced Apple Glaze or Apple Cider Molasses

Preheat oven to 350°F. Spray a baking dish with non-stick cooking spray. Try to pick a pan about the same size as the four chops laid out flat. Dump the prepared dressing into the pan and smooth the top. Lay chops on top of the dressing. Sprinkle with salt and pepper. If desired, place sliced apples on top of the chop. You may also glaze the chops if you like. Bake 20–30 minutes or until they reach an internal temperature of 165°F. The cooking time will vary with the thickness of the chop.

Makes 4 servings.

Meatloaf

Meatloaf is the essence of what we now call comfort food. This is another of those recipes which have a million variations. Therefore, I'll give you my basic meatloaf and you can take it from there.

This recipe will make a nice size meatloaf for one meal. Feel free to double it if you like cold meatloaf sandwiches, which I do.

Meatloaf is an easy recipe to teach a young cook. They may need help with the chopping if they do not have knife skills yet, but the rest is pure kid fun. Make sure they use disposable gloves or thoroughly wash their hands before they mix the ingredients.

1 egg
1 cup breadcrumbs
2 tablespoons parsley
2 tablespoons steak sauce
1 tablespoon Worcestershire sauce
dash Tabasco sauce
1 pound ground beef
salt and pepper to taste
1/2 cup finely chopped onion
1 clove of garlic, peeled and minced

(Optional ingredients: grated cheese, oregano, thyme, barbeque sauce, red pepper. You may also mix other ground meats including pork, veal and bulk sausage meat.)

Preheat oven to 350°F. Spray a loaf pan with non-stick cooking spray.

Combine all ingredients above in a large mixing bowl. Hands work best for this. Mix until just well combined; you don't want to overdo the mixing.

Check the mixture for moistness. Depending on your meat and what ingredients you use you may have to adjust the moisture content. It should not seem "wet" or "dry". I take a clump in my hands and pull it apart. If it seems gooey, I'll add some breadcrumbs. If it looks dry, add some milk or more of a sauce if you're using one or even another egg. After a couple of tries, you'll develop a feel for how it should look.

If you want to check seasonings, pinch off a small bit of the mixture and cook in a frying pan.

Press the meat mixture into the prepared loaf pan. Bake 30–40 minutes or until it reaches an internal temperature of 165°F.

Let meatloaf sit for a few minutes before slicing.

When I make meat loaf, I have to have baked potatoes and green beans; they just seem to go together.

Makes 4 servings.

 # Chicken

Once an expensive and special food, chicken has become a universal component of almost every menu. Chicken lends itself to so many preparations that entire cookbooks are devoted to the bird. I'll keep it simple with a few basic dishes.

Buy your favorite chicken parts, a whole cut up bird, or cut it up yourself. Kids seem to love the drumsticks. Thighs are less expensive than other parts and have a very nice flavor. Of course breasts are the most expensive, though wings have now become the next most expensive part. Keep your eyes open for sales. Certain parts and whole birds can often be found for less than a dollar a pound. However, if you want to splurge, look for pasture-raised birds at your local farm market. These chickens have a flavor noticeably more complex than a store bought bird and also are richer in desirable nutrients.

❦ Baked Chicken Parts ❦

Baked chicken is one of the easiest suppers to make. Put the pieces in a roasting pan and pop into the oven. Could anything be simpler?

Kids can be taught how to handle poultry properly in this recipe. Stress proper sanitation. It is also a chance to teach a bit of chicken anatomy and the basics of how to roast.

salt and pepper
1 whole chicken cut up, or your favorite assortment of legs, thighs, breasts, wings
Allens Hill Farm Apple Cider Molasses, Smokey or Spiced Apple Glaze (optional)

Preheat oven to 400°F. Rinse the chicken pieces, pat dry and place skin side up on a roasting pan, preferable with a rack. Sprinkle with salt and pepper to taste. Put into oven and bake 20–40 minutes or more depending on the size of the parts. If the skin becomes too brown, either reduce the heat, or cover loosely with foil. Check with a thermometer to make sure it reaches an internal temperature of 165°F. If using a glaze, brush on about 10 minutes before removing from the oven.

Makes 4 servings.

🌾 Chicken and Stuffing 🌾

This is a case where a package of store bought stuffing mix makes life easy.

salt and pepper
1 package of chicken stuffing mix or see Stuffing recipe on page 108
1 whole chicken cut up, or your favorite assortment of legs, thighs, breasts, wings

Preheat oven to 350°F. Prepare stuffing mix according to the directions on the package. Spray a baking dish with non-stick cooking spray. Put stuffing into pan and smooth. Rinse the chicken pieces, pat dry and place skin side up on the stuffing. Sprinkle with salt and pepper to taste. Put into oven and bake about 40 minutes or more depending on the size of the parts. If the skin becomes too brown, either reduce the heat, or cover loosely with foil. Check with a thermometer to make sure it reaches an internal temperature of 165°F.

Makes 4 to 6 servings.

🌾 Sautéed Chicken Breasts 🌾

There are a lot of options to dress up a basic sautéed chicken breast. This is an excellent dish to use your imagination and creativity. Following the basic recipe below, I'll offer up a few ideas of my own.

There are two options when sautéing the chicken. You can either cook the breasts as is, or coat with flour. If you are serving the chicken plain, I would probably skip the flour. However, if you plan on adding a sauce, I would dust with flour. The chicken stays moist and the sauce will adhere better to the chicken.

salt and pepper to taste
4 boneless chicken breasts
2 tablespoons vegetable or olive oil
1 cup flour, or breadcrumbs (optional)

Put a large skillet on medium high heat. Pat breasts dry with a paper towel. When pan is hot, add oil. Season the breast and put in pan. Cook about 4 minutes or so per side, until they begin to brown and reach as internal temperature of 165°F.

If you are coating the breasts, season the flour or breadcrumbs with salt and pepper. Dredge the chicken and shake off any excess. Place in the skillet and cook as above.

Makes 4 servings.

Quick Sauce

You can make a simple sauce by simply deglazing the pan with water, stock, wine or a combination of both. Simply place the pan back on the heat and add liquid. Scrape the bottom of the pan to deglaze and let boil vigorously until the liquid is reduced by about half. You can add a pat of butter or a little bit of cream to bring the sauce together if you like. Or add some fresh squeezed lemon juice. Spoon over the chicken.

Variation

Chicken and Mushrooms. After you remove the chicken from the pan, add a couple of tablespoons of butter and one cup of sliced mushrooms. Add a clove of minced garlic and some parsley if you wish. Cook a few minutes until mushrooms become tender and release their moisture. Add a couple of tablespoons of wine, cook another minute or two. Spoon over the chicken.

"Oven Fried" Chicken
Parts, Breasts, Fingers & Nuggets

This is a great substitute for traditional fried chicken. Breading the chicken and baking it eliminates all the added fat (and mess) of traditional fried chicken. You can use this technique for chicken parts, boneless breasts, fresh chicken tenders, of you can even make your own chicken nuggets. The process is the same; just adjust the cooking length based on the type of chicken you are cooking.

1 cut up chicken, or assorted chicken parts, or 4 chicken breasts, or fresh chicken tenders, or 4 chicken breasts cut into 1-1/2-inch chunks.

2 eggs	*1 cup flour*
1 cup milk	*pepper to taste*
4 cups bread crumbs	*dash of cayenne pepper*
1 teaspoon seasoned salt	*2 teaspoons poultry seasoning*

Preheat oven to 425°F. You need three dishes for this method: a bowl containing the flour for the first step; a bowl in which you beat the egg and then beat in the milk to make the egg wash, for the second step; a bowl containing your breading and seasonings, for the third step. Pat the chicken dry with a paper towel. Dust the chicken parts in flour. Then dip into the second bowl and coat with egg wash. Remove and place into the breading and coat completely. Put onto baking sheet.

When all the chicken is breaded, place it into the oven. Bake until it's a nice golden brown and the chicken reaches an internal temperature of 165°F. Nuggets or tenders should take about 15 minutes, breasts 20–25 minutes, bone-in parts 25–35 minutes. Serve with oven fries or smashed potatoes and a hot vegetable.

Makes 4 servings.

Chicken Parmesan

1 cup pasta sauce
4 boneless chicken breasts
1/4 cup grated parmesan
1 cup shredded mozzarella.

Preheat the oven to 350°F.

Follow direction above for either oven baked chicken breasts or sautéed breasts using breadcrumbs. Place the breasts in a baking dish. Spoon some pasta sauce over the top. Add grated parmesan cheese to shredded mozzarella. Spread cheese over top of breasts. Sprinkle with some oregano is you like. Place in the upper third of the oven and bake until cheese is nicely melted.

Serve with a side of pasta and sauce, tossed salad and garlic bread.

Have the novice cook assemble this one. They can make the call on when it's done by looking at the cheese on top.

Makes 4 servings.

Dukkah Chicken Breasts
Recipe on page 95

Seafood

❧ Broiled Fish Fillet ☙

Fish is an excellent change of pace for supper. It was a regular on Fridays as a kid in our home. Fish fillets are simple and very quick to cook.

There are many varieties to choose from. Fresh frozen are less expensive and in many cases every bit as good as fresh. Cod, haddock, flounder, tilapia, mahi mahi and catfish are readily available.

Old Bay Seasoning
butter-flavored non-stick cooking spray
6 ounces of fish per person you will be serving (approx.)

Preheat oven to 500°F. Put rack into the upper third of the oven. Place fish onto a baking pan (a pie tin works great also). Spray with butter spray and lightly season with Old Bay. Put about one-eighth inch of water onto pan, being careful not to wash off seasoning. Place in oven and cook until done. "If it's white, it's right" is what I was taught. Once the fillet turns from translucent to white and flaky, it's done. Take care not to over-cook. Cooking time can vary from 5 to over 10 minutes depending on the thickness of the fish. Serve with lemon and tartar sauce.

Makes 4 servings.

Variations

❧ Cajun Broiled Fish: substitute Cajun seasoning for Old Bay and cook as directed above.

❧ Crumb-Topped Fish: mix about one-half cup of breadcrumbs or fresh cracker crumbs with two tablespoons of butter and one teaspoon of Old Bay Seasoning. Spray fish with butter spray and top with crumb mixture. Cook as directed above, being careful not to burn the crumb topping.

❧ Oven-Fried Fish ☙

Follow the directions above for oven-fried chicken. Simply substitute Old Bay Seasoning for poultry seasoning. Reduce to cooking time to 10–15 minutes depending on the thickness of the fillet.

Dukkah Broiled Fish

Dukkah is a Middle Eastern blend of ground nuts, spices and sesame seeds. Typically, it is eaten by dipping bread into oil and then into the dukkah. It also makes an outstanding topping for fish.

Try Allens Hill Farm Dukkah. See the Ingredient Suppliers section on page 181 to find out how to order.

butter, oil, or cooking spray
Allens Hill Farm Down Under Dukkah
Your favorite fish fillet or steak: 6–8 ounces per person

Preheat oven to 450°F with rack in top third of oven. Spray roasting pan and place fish into pan. Brush fish with melted butter, oil or spray with cooking spray. Sprinkle on Dukkah to coat. Add about one-eighth inch of water to roasting pan being careful not to wash off topping. Cook until fish is done. (Firm to touch, flaky, no longer translucent; "white is right"). Thin fillets like tilapia will take only a few minutes. Thicker fillets and steaks may take 10 minutes or more. (Check thicker fillets for internal temp of 165°F).

Beer Batter Fish Fry

One of the great traditions in upstate New York is the Friday fish fry. This is the outgrowth of the Catholic observance of meatless Fridays in this heavily Catholic area. Go to almost any restaurant, tavern or even firehouse on Fridays, order the fish fry and you'll get a huge piece of beer battered haddock that is bigger than the plate, a mountain of French fries and a scoop of coleslaw.

This batter is also great for onion rings or for any fried vegetables like mushrooms, broccoli, cauliflower or zucchini.

1 cup beer
1 teaspoon salt
1/8 teaspoon pepper
1 cup all-purpose flour
dash cayenne pepper
1 tablespoon vegetable oil
1 teaspoon baking powder
1/4 teaspoon garlic powder
4–8 ounce skin-on haddock fillets

Heat your deep fryer to 365°F. In a mixing bowl combine the dry ingredients. Add oil and beer and mix until smooth. Dry the haddock fillets with a paper towel and dip one at a time into the batter. Remove battered fillet from bowl and allow excess batter to run off. Gently lay fillet into oil being careful not to burn yourself with the oil (using tongs will reduce this risk). Fry each fillet until golden brown and the fish reaches an internal temperature of 165°F. Place cooked fillet on absorbent paper to drain.

Makes 4 servings.

Breakfast Supper

A fun change of pace is to have a "breakfast" supper. When I was a kid, we did this frequently. It's an opportunity to have a meatless meal or a very economical one.

You can also have a very hearty supper if you include breakfast meats and sides like home fries.

I won't list recipes here. Simply refer to the chapter on breakfast for all sorts of ideas.

Give breakfast supper a try. I think you'll like it.

Belgian Waffles
Recipe on page 38

Grill It

Grilling is a rite of summer in the Northeast. In other parts of the country the grill is always ready to be fired up. Any time you can break out the grill is a good time. A stovetop grill pan is a reasonable substitute. These are just a few ideas for supper items.

GRILLED MARINATED STEAK

You can also call this London Broil. I just call it good eatin'. I like to buy whole sirloins at my wholesale club. You can't beat the value. I always cut a few one-inch thick steaks and freeze them. To make a great steak, I simply thaw the beef and throw the marinade right in the zip lock bag I froze the steak in. When it's supper time, just toss it on the grill. The marinade is an opportunity to exercise your creativity. Mine changes depending on my mood and what I have at hand.

one-inch thick steak: sirloin, London broil, flank steak or your favorite cut

1/2 cup oil
1/4 cup vinegar
1 tablespoon parsley flakes
1/4 teaspoon red pepper flakes
1/2 teaspoon sesame oil (optional)
1 teaspoon salt
1/2 teaspoon thyme
freshly ground black pepper
2 tablespoons finely chopped onion
2 cloves of garlic peeled and minced
2 teaspoons Worcestershire sauce (opt)

Put all ingredients together in a small bowl. Stir together and put in bag with the steak. Refrigerate and marinate at least one hour, preferably several.

Grill steak to desired doneness. Let rest on a cutting board for several minutes. Slice across the grain in thin strips.

Makes 4 servings.

Variation

Redneck Style: you can cook the steak above or any steak without a grill if you have either a real charcoal (not briquette) fire or a wood fire. When the coals are nice and hot, you can lay the steak directly on the coals. Cook about 4 minutes per side for a one-inch thick steak. Remove from coals, brush off any pieces of coals that may adhere to steak and let rest about ten minutes before cutting. The flavor is really great.

Burgers, Hot Dogs and Sausages

I know, I know. Do I really have to talk about how to grill burgers and hot dogs? Well, I actually do have a few words of wisdom on the subject.

If you are going to serve hot dogs, take my advice and spend the extra dollar or two and get good quality dogs. I like the natural, skin on varieties that burst open and snap when you bite into them. If you have a local producer, it's probably a good choice to go with that brand. Every region has its unique blend of meats and seasonings. I like to cook them over a lower heat and cover the grill to get a nice even browning.

You can add some real variety to your grill by choosing different sausages. Supermarkets are carrying an ever increasing selection of sausage types and flavors. If you have a good local meat market, check out what they have to offer. Some are great on a bun. Others are excellent to serve plated with some fresh sweet corn and oven fries.

Good burgers start with good meat. Buy the best ground beef you can afford. Often I can find sirloin or chuck on sale and grind it myself. If your meat is too lean, your burgers will be dry. Avoid frozen patties; in most cases they are fattier, lack flavor and are tough.

I think it's important to season the burgers. I always use grill seasoning. See the Pantry Checklist section for the recipe, on page 175. Season both sides. Flip the burgers when juice starts to form on the top. If you are adding cheese, do so shortly after flipping. For safety, always have a thermometer at hand and make sure the burgers are cooked to 165°F.

A great burger is finished off by finding a home in a nice fresh bun and having a nice selection of toppings. Tomato slices, fresh lettuce, sliced pickles, sautéed mushrooms, thinly sliced onions, ketchup, mustard, and steak sauce are all good ways to make the perfect burger.

In this area, local burger joints always serve burgers topped with a spicy, meat sauce. It's really quite good. You can find the recipe on page 50.

Chicken

Grilled chicken is an outdoor cooking staple. Of course you can grill chicken in several ways for supper. Boneless skinless breasts or skin on parts all make outstanding meals. I'll give a couple of suggestions, but please use your own creativity.

Boneless breasts are quick and versatile. They make a meal as is, or can be used on a salad. Marinate before grilling or glaze afterwards with Allens Hill Farm Smokey Apple Glaze.

Smokey Glazed BBQ Chicken

1/3 cup BBQ Rub
1/2 cup vegetable or olive oil
Allens Hill Farm Smokey Apple Glaze
2 chickens split into halves or quarters

for BBQ Rub

2 tablespoons paprika	*2 tablespoons kosher salt*
1 teaspoon black pepper	*2 tablespoons brown sugar*
2 tablespoons chili powder	*1/4 teaspoon cayenne pepper*
1-1/2 teaspoons onion powder	*2 tablespoons granulated garlic*

Mix together BBQ Rub ingredients (store any unused rub in an airtight container).

Mix the BBQ rub with the oil. Massage this mixture onto the chicken. If not cooking right away, cover with plastic wrap and refrigerate. I like to do this several hours ahead to let the BBQ rub really flavor the chicken. You can intensify the effect of the rub by getting it under the skin.

Grill directly over a fairly slow fire, about 325°F. Start the chicken skin up, close the lid and let cook about 25 minutes. Turn over, cover and let cook about 20 minutes more, checking the make sure the fire is not too hot and burning the skin. When you reach a minimum internal temp of 165°F, turn the chicken skin side up and brush with Smokey Apple Glaze. Either let cook a few more minutes as is, or turn over to caramelize the glaze. Watch carefully as the high sugar content of the glaze make for quick browning if the fire is too hot.

Makes 8 servings.

Grilled Chicken with Cornell Marinade

During the summertime in the Finger Lakes, you'll see columns of smoke rising from local volunteer fire departments and county fairs. The delicious aromas are from chicken barbeques. The chicken they cook is marinated in Cornell Marinade. It is simple and so very good.

Cornell Marinade was developed by Robert C. Baker, Professor of Poultry Science and Food Science at Cornell. He also created the chicken nugget. This is enough marinade for several chickens.

Cornell Chicken Barbecue Sauce/Finger Lakes Marinade Recipe
(Adapted from the Cornell University website)

1 egg
1/2 cup cooking oil
2 cups cider vinegar
1/2 teaspoon pepper
1-1/2 tablespoons salt
2 teaspoons poultry seasoning

Beat the egg in a mixing bowl. Add the oil and beat again. Add other ingredients and stir.

Cut chicken into quarters. Pour marinade over chicken; marinate overnight.

Grill chicken slowly, brushing on additional marinade. Cook until the chicken reaches an internal temperature of 165°F and the skin is a nice golden brown.

Grilled Chicken Breasts

One of the easiest and most versatile items to grill are boneless chicken breasts. Grill without seasoning; instead, glaze or marinate ahead of time.

Grilled chicken breasts can be sliced and put over a salad or served with fresh vegetables.

Try the following marinades.

French Apple Dressing and Marinade
(recipe on page 176 in the Pantry Checklist section)

Stir-Fry Marinade
(recipe on page 62)

Your favorite Italian dressing

Glaze with Allens Hill Farm Apple Cider Molasses or
Allens Hill Farm Smokey Apple Glaze

Chops

Chops are one of the easiest items to grill. Pork would be the most common, but lamb chops are a real treat.

I like to season the chops lightly with grill seasoning. If you like to add some variety, finish with some Allens Hill Farm Smokey apple glaze or spiced apple glaze.

Seafood

Seafood is a bit pricey for supper on a regular basis, however, it does add variety, great nutrition and flavor.

When grilling fish, choose either steak cuts or firm, thick fillets. Swordfish, tuna and halibut are great on the grill. Salmon steaks or fillets work well. If you are skilled, more delicate fillets can be attempted, but make sure you have a very clean and well seasoned grill.

I like to use a grill basting sauce to add flavor as well as seasoning with Old Bay.

Skewered shrimp or scallops are a real treat on the grill. Even lobster tails can be grilled. The flavor is amazing. Just take care not to overcook. Remember, "white is right".

Grilled salmon is outstanding with Allens Hill Farm Smokey Apple Glaze.

Grill Basting Sauce for Seafood

Melt 4 tablespoons of margarine. Add one-half teaspoon of Old Bay seasoning and 1 tablespoon of white wine.

When cooking seafood, brush lightly with the basting sauce. Sprinkle lightly with Old Bay. If the fillet has skin, start skin side down. You should score the skin with shallow cuts about two inches apart to prevent curling. When you see beads of moisture on the top side and the color of the fish has changed about half way through the fillet, brush with basting sauce and season. Flip the seafood and finish cooking.

Dinner Salads

I'm not sure that a recipe is really required for a dinner salad. I include it with the list of supper items since you can put together a wonderful dinner salad in minutes.

A salad can be just the ticket on a really hot day or when a full meal just seems like too much food.

The key to a great salad is a foundation of great greens. See my dissertation on salad greens in the Side Dish section, page 114. Once you have that, just have some fun. I find the best salads are a symphony of contrasting flavors, textures, colors, even between hot and cold items. I'll provide a list of ingredients that are great on salads.

You still need a dressing to bring it all together. I'll provide a couple of scratch dressing recipes, but any store bought dressing you like is just fine. When making a dinner salad, keep a couple of things in mind. A wonderfully healthy and low calorie salad can be destroyed with too much rich dressing. Think about a low fat or fat free dressing if you are concerned about calories.

It's also about how much dressing you use. Less is more. Use half of your normal amount of dressing and thoroughly toss the dressing to completely coat the salad. You'll find that the flavor is better with much less dressing. It's healthier and you'll save a lot of money on dressing.

Finish off your dinner salad with some nice fresh bread or garlic bread.

Since there are really no rules to salad making, this can be good kid fun. Let them select the vegetables. Show them how to clean and prepare the greens and vegetables. Then give them free reign to assemble and arrange to plate. Discuss presentation and how to make it look attractive.

Meats

Almost any cooked meat works on a salad. It can be hot or cold. Beef, ham, lamb, pork all work well.

Poultry

Chicken is the most common protein to find on a dinner salad. It can be freshly grilled, cooked or even fried. Chicken salad can even be put on a dinner salad. Any other cooked poultry is certainly fine as well.

Seafood

Freshly grilled or cooked cocktail shrimp make an elegant salad. Freshly grilled tuna is outstanding. There are so many varieties of seafood…be creative!

Tofu

For vegetarians looking to add some substance to a dinner salad, cubes or strips of tofu are an excellent option.

Cheese

Cheese can either be a garnish or a main ingredient. Freshly grated cheese over the top of the salad adds interest. Strips or cubes of cheddar, Swiss, mozzarella, jack or any of your favorite cheeses are excellent as well.

Vegetables

There are all types of raw veggies that can be added to a dinner salad. Just use what you like. I also love grilled vegetables on my salads. The flavor is great; they add a different texture and the contrast of something warm with an ice cold salad is wonderful. Zucchini, other types of summer squash are good choices. Give eggplant a try. See page 111.

Fresh Fruit

Fresh fruit is a way to add flavor and color contrast to a salad. It also gives an opportunity to balance some of the saltiness of the meats and dressings with the sweetness of the fruit. Fruit is a good way to add additional nutrition.

Dried Fruit

I love raisins on my salads. There are many other dried fruits to choose from. They have concentrated flavors and again add a lovely contrasting sweetness.

Crunch

A bit of crunch adds interest to a salad. The most common choice is croutons. Store bought croutons come in a variety of flavors. However, I found one way to get my family interested in eating salads was to make fresh croutons. They are quick and easy to make. Not to mention, an excellent way to get rid of stale bread. I always have to make a double batch since half of them get snatched before they even get to the salad.

Croutons

salt
1 teaspoon garlic powder
1/2 teaspoon parsley flakes
4 tablespoons butter or margarine
4 slices bread or leftover buns or rolls

Cut the bread into one-inch squares. Melt the butter in a skillet over medium high heat. Add bread and stir or toss to coat with butter. Sprinkle with garlic powder, parsley and a little salt. Cook, stirring croutons frequently until they are lightly browned and crunchy.

Add some fun and crunch with corn chips, tortilla chips or Chinese noodles. I enjoy sunflower seeds with my salads. Other nuts like almonds, pecans and walnuts are great as well.

Dinner: Formal Meals and Holiday Celebrations

When I was growing up, dinner was the big meal of the week on Sunday afternoons or at the holidays. The main course was usually a roast of pork, beef or ham. Mashed potatoes, at least a couple of vegetables and bread were served alongside. The meal was always followed by a pie or cake.

Holidays of course were more elaborate with an array of pre-meal snacks, a wider variety of side dishes and special desserts.

Classic Roasted Chicken

I never roasted chickens whole until recently. I guess I had been brought up just cooking the parts; they cook more quickly and are "ready to serve" when they come out of the oven; no carving required. However, a whole roasted chicken is a beautiful presentation, has a wonderfully crisp skin and stays very moist. It does take a bit longer to cook and requires carving, but it's worth the extra effort. This version is very basic; no herbs or stuffing. Feel free to add if you like.

This recipe also makes a nice formal dinner item, especially if you splurge for a free range bird and add stuffing or herb butter.

vegetable oil
1 whole roasting chicken, about 4 pounds
kosher salt and fresh ground pepper to taste
Allens Hill Farm Apple Cider Molasses (optional)

Preheat oven to 425°F. Rinse the bird inside and out. Remove any lumps of fat. To make it easier to carve, remove the wishbone. Run a sharp knife along both sides of the wishbone. When it is free from the meat pull it out. Also cut off the tips of the wings at the first joint.

To properly roast the chicken, you want to truss it up. Take a few feet of butcher's twine and slip it under the back of the chicken near the tail. Bring it up and over the ends of the drumsticks, cross it and pull it back down, drawing the legs together and closing the cavity. Draw the twine back along the sides pinning the wings to the side and then tie off the twine to hold everything in place.

To cook the bird, you will need a roasting pan or, what I like is a cast iron skillet or Dutch oven. Put a little bit of oil in the bottom of the pan. Pat the chicken dry and sprinkle salt and freshly ground pepper. Set the chicken in the pan on its side. Roast for 25 minutes.

Turn the chicken onto its other side and roast another 25 minutes. Next turn the chicken breast side up baste and reduce the heat to 400°F. Roast another 20 minutes or until a thermometer inserted into the breast reaches an internal temperature of 165°F. Remove chicken and let rest on cutting board for at least 10 minutes before carving.

Optional: Brush chicken with apple cider molasses to glaze and return to oven for a few more minutes.

Makes 4 servings.

Potato Crusted Chicken Breasts

The shredded potatoes keep the chicken moist and add a wonderful crunchy texture. This dish works equally well with a nice firm fish. I like to use Idaho potatoes, but sweet potatoes work great as well.

4 chicken breasts
olive oil for frying
salt and pepper to taste
Cajun Dipping Sauce (recipe on page 168)
1–2 potatoes (enough to yield two cups)

Inspect chicken breasts. If over one-half inch think, pound out until one-half inch thick.

Wash potatoes. Shred into bowl. Put large skillet on stove and preheat on medium high. Spread each breast with Cajun sauce. Grab some shredded spuds and put into a paper towel. Squeeze to remove as much water as possible. Press onto breast, then sprinkle with salt and fresh ground pepper. Add olive oil. Put a shred of potato in pan. When it sizzles, place chicken potato side down into pan, pressing gently. After 2-3 minutes, flip potatoes when they are nicely golden brown.

Cook until chicken is 165°F internal temperature.

Makes 4 servings.

Quick and Easy to Carve Turkey with Sausage Stuffing

We're not a big turkey family but when I do a turkey, this is my favorite version. It has the merits of being simple to carve, since it's essentially boneless. It also cooks in a fraction of the time of a whole stuffed bird. Throw the bones into a pot with some water to get a start on your turkey soup. If you prefer another type of stuffing feel free to substitute. This one is very good and very quick and easy to make.

Italian Sausage Stuffing

1 cup sour cream
4 cups breadcrumbs
salt and pepper to taste
1 cup fresh minced parsley
3 cups minced onions
2 cloves garlic, minced
1/4 cup butter (1/2 stick)
1-1/2 pounds sweet Italian sausage

Remove the casing from the sausage and put into a skillet. Cook over medium heat, breaking the sausage into rough chunks. When cooked, put the sausage into a mixing bowl. Without draining the juices, add butter, onions and garlic to the skillet. Cook 8-10 minutes until onions are soft. Dump into bowl with sausage. Add the remaining ingredients and combine. Season with salt and pepper to taste.

The Turkey

10-12 pound turkey
5 cups stuffing (your choice)
1/4 cup (half stick) melted butter
kosher salt and fresh ground pepper

Bone the turkey by starting in the neck area. Cut out the wishbone using a boning knife. With the turkey breast side down, cut along the whole length of the backbone. Carefully scrape along the rib bones, being careful not to penetrate the skin, first one side and then the other up to but not over the top of the breastbone. Cut through the ball joints holding the wings and thighs to the carcass. When both sides are done, lift up the carcass and carefully scrape along the breastbone to release the carcass without cutting through the skin. Flip over so the bird is skin side up and remove the thigh bones. Remove the wing nubbins.

Preheat the oven to 350°F. Mound the stuffing on a baking sheet. Liberally salt and pepper the underside of the turkey and place skin side up over the stuffing. Brush the skin with melted butter then sprinkle with salt and pepper. Roast 1-1/2–2 hours, basting every 20 minutes until the thickest part of the breast reaches 165°F. Remove from oven and let rest before carving.

Transfer bird to a cutting board and stuffing to a serving dish. Simply cut off the drumsticks and wings then slice right through the rest of the boneless bird.

Makes 6 to 8 servings.

Cornish Game Hens with Cornbread Pecan and Sausage Stuffing

This is a great entrée for a dinner party or family gathering. Half a bird is an ample portion. The stuffing is a lovely combination of flavors and textures. For the cornbread, use the recipe on page 146.

salt and pepper to taste
2 Rock Cornish game hens
2 tablespoons melted butter
cornbread, pecan and sausage stuffing
1/4 cup Allens Hill Farm Apple Cider Molasses

Stuffing

1/2 cup (1 stick) butter
salt and pepper to taste
4 cups cornbread, crumbled
1/2 cup finely chopped celery
1/2 cup of pecan pieces
1 teaspoon rubbed sage
1 small onion, finely chopped
1 pound bulk breakfast sausage

Put cornbread into mixing bowl. Cook sausage into a sauté pan and break into clumps, cooking over medium heat until done. Spoon out sausage. Add butter to pan with sausage drippings. Sauté the onions and celery in the butter until they are soft. Pour into mixing bowl. Add pecans. Add salt and pepper to taste. Mix until well combined.

Preheat oven to 400°F. Split game hens in half. Salt and pepper the undersides. Divide the stuffing into four mounds on a baking sheet. Place hens skin side up on stuffing. Brush skin with melted butter and sprinkle with salt and pepper. Put into oven for 15 minutes, and then reduce heat to 325°F. Roast another 30–40 minutes or until hens reach an internal temperature of 150°F. Brush hens with Allens Hill Farm Apple Cider Molasses. Return to oven and continue to cook until they reach 165°F.

Makes 4 servings.

Dukkah Stuffed Chicken Breasts

salt and pepper
cooked orso pasta
butter, oil or non-stick cooking spray
boneless chicken breasts (one per person)
Allens Hill Farm Dukkah (use your favorite flavor)
Allens Hill Farm Apple Cider Molasses or Smokey Apple Glaze (optional)

Preheat oven to 400°F or fire up your grill. Lay a chicken breast flat on a cutting board and carefully fillet open the breast by slicing parallel to the cutting board. Do not cut all the way through. You want to be able to open up the breast like a book. Lay the chicken open. Sprinkle with dukkah. Roll up the breast and tuck the seam underneath. If grilling, use a toothpick or two to keep it together.

If roasting, spray roasting pan with cooking spray and place breast seam side down. Brush with butter, oil or spray with cooking spray. Salt and pepper. Cook about 30 minutes until you reach an internal temperature of 165°F. If using molasses or glaze, brush on now. Remove from oven and let stand for a few minutes. Slice across the roll and serve on bed of cooked orso.

Chicken Breasts Stuffed with Mushrooms and Raisins

This dish is actually quite easy to prepare. It is a wonderfully flavorful and elegant way to perk up a bland chicken breast. The savory dressing is made slightly sweet with the addition of the raisins.

Chicken and Stuffing

1/4 cup raisins	3 tablespoons butter
dash of cayenne pepper	salt and pepper to taste
1 tablespoon white wine	2 tablespoons sour cream
2 tablespoons breadcrumbs	1 tablespoon chopped parsley
1/8 teaspoon poultry seasoning	2 boneless skinless chicken breasts

1-1/2 cups thinly sliced mushrooms

Breading

1 egg	1/2 cup milk
1/2 cup flour	1 cup breadcrumbs
salt and pepper to taste	1/2 teaspoon poultry seasoning

Preheat oven to 450°F. Add butter to sauté pan over medium heat. Coarsely chop sliced mushrooms and add to pan. While mushrooms are cooking, chop raisins. When mushrooms have released their moisture, add white wine. Cook until most of the liquid is gone. Remove from heat and add remaining ingredients. Using a sharp, thin bladed knife, cut a pocket into the chicken breast. Divide the stuffing in half and fill each pocket with half of the stuffing. Close the opening with a toothpick or small metal skewer.

Set up three bowls. In the first put the flour. In the second, beat together the egg and milk. In the third mix the breadcrumbs, poultry seasoning, salt and pepper. Dust each breast in the flour, then dip in the egg wash and finally coat completely in the breadcrumbs. Place into a baking pan. Place in preheated oven for 25–35 minutes or until internal temperature reaches 165°F.

Makes 2 servings.

GRILLED LAMB CHOPS WITH GLAZED & ROASTED PEACHES

1 teaspoon salt
1 teaspoon pepper
1 tablespoon lemon juice
2 tablespoons fresh rosemary
1/2 cup olive oil
2 frenched lamb racks
2 cloves garlic, minced
1 tablespoon balsamic vinegar

With a sharp knife, cut between the bones of the lamb to make chops. Put into a large Ziploc bag. Mix remaining ingredients to make the marinade and pour over lamb. Close bag and refrigerate. Let marinate for a few hours or, preferably, overnight.

When ready to serve, remove chops from the marinade, brushing off excess marinade and herbs. Grill for about 3 minutes per side at medium high heat. Chops should be medium rare, 135°F. Don't overcook.

Serve with grilled peaches.

Peaches

4 fresh peaches, halved, peeled and pitted
1/2 cup Allens Hill Farm Apple Cider Molasses

Brush peaches with apple cider molasses and place on a sheet tray in a 350°F oven. Roast 10–15 minutes or until peaches become tender and caramelized.

Makes 2 servings.

HERB CRUSTED ROAST BEEF WITH MUSHROOMS

There are numerous cuts of beef that make great roasts. Higher quality parts of the beef are more expensive. Top or bottom round or sirloin roasts tend to be pretty middle of the road as far as cost. If you cook it right, you'll have a moist and tender roast. That means slow roasting.

herb rub
one beef roast
sautéed mushrooms
1 bottle steak sauce

Herb Rub

1 teaspoon thyme
1 teaspoon onion powder
2 tablespoons coarse sea salt
2 teaspoons granulated garlic
1 tablespoon coarse ground pepper

Mix all herb rub ingredients together and set aside.

Preheat the oven to 275°F. Put the roast in a roasting pan. Slather steak sauce over the roast to cover it completely. Sprinkle herb rub over roast and rub it in. Place roast in oven. Figure about 25 minutes per pound.

Cook to about 135°F for medium rare. Let rest 10–15 minutes before carving. Plate and spoon mushrooms over the top of the beef.

Sautéed Mushrooms

2 tablespoons parsley
salt and pepper to taste
1-1/2 pounds of mushrooms
2 cloves garlic, minced
1/4 cup (1/2 stick) butter
2 tablespoons vermouth or white wine

Thickly slice mushrooms. Melt butter in skillet. Add mushrooms and cook over medium until moisture begins to come out of the mushrooms. Add garlic, salt, pepper to taste and parsley. Cook a few minutes and add wine. Continue to cook until mushrooms are just tender.

Makes 6-8 servings depending on the size of the roast.

Pork with Apple Onion Glaze

1 pork roast (any cut is fine)

salt and pepper
1/2 teaspoon thyme
1 tablespoon parsley
1/8 teaspoon cayenne
2 tablespoons butter
1 cup minced onions
1 garlic clove, minced
1/4 teaspoon cinnamon
1/2 cup Allens Hill Farm Apple Cider Molasses

Preheat oven to 450°F. Mince one onion (about one cup). Cook in a small saucepan with the butter until very soft. Add seasonings and Allens Hill Farm Apple Cider Molasses. Bring to a boil then simmer for 5 minutes.

Use a blender to puree the onions and make a semi-smooth sauce. Place roast into pan and sprinkle with salt and pepper. Put roast into oven for about 15 minutes. Remove roast and reduce heat to 325°F. Brush on sauce and place back into the oven.

Brush on additional sauce every 15 minutes until the pork reaches an internal temperature of 150°F. Let rest for at least 10 minutes before carving.

Garnish with remaining sauce if desired.

Makes 6 to 8 servings (depending on the size of the roast).

Baked Ham with Spiced Apple Glaze

1 fully cooked bone in or boneless ham
1 jar Allens Hill Farm Spiced Apple Glaze

Preheat oven to 350°F. Put ham in roasting pan. Bake about 10 minutes per pound until internal temperature reaches 150°F. Remove from oven.

Brush with spiced apple glaze. Return to oven and bake until ham reaches 165°F.

Makes 8 to 10 servings (depending on the size of the ham).

Grilled Salmon with Allens Hill Farm Smokey Apple Glaze

This recipe will also work with any fish that is firm enough to grill; tuna, swordfish, grouper, shark are all good options.

Old Bay Seasoning
Allens Hill Farm Smokey Apple Glaze
one 6–8 ounce salmon fillet per person

Grill Basting Sauce

1 tablespoon white wine
1 teaspoon Old Bay Seasoning
1/4 cup of melted butter or margarine

Prepare the salmon by scoring the skin.

Brush the fillet with basting sauce and sprinkle lightly with Old Bay. Place skin side up on grill. After about one minute "shuffle" fillet to prevent sticking.

When fillet is cooked about half through, baste and sprinkle with Old Bay. Flip and brush with Allens Hill Farm Smokey Apple Glaze.

Cook until 165°F internal temperature.

Garnish with lemon.

Crepes with Fresh Greens

This is also a great brunch item.

12 eggs
salt and pepper to taste
fresh minced garlic to taste
fresh herbs (dill, parsley, etc)
4 tablespoons butter or olive oil
12 Buckwheat Crepes
(keep warm in 200°F oven)
(for recipe, see page 36)
4 cups of your favorite greens chopped
(lettuce, spinach, endive, romaine, kale, etc)

Sautee greens and garlic in 2 tablespoon butter with a bit of salt until greens are wilted. Scramble eggs. Drain pan, add remaining butter to pan and melt. Add eggs and herbs. Cook eggs until moist. Salt and pepper to taste. Roll into warm crepes and serve immediately.

Makes 6 servings.

Finger Lakes Locavore Quiche

If you want to make a simple but elegant dinner using all local ingredients, quiche is a perfect dish to prepare. A trip to your farmers market can provide your ingredients as well as greens for a salad, a fresh baked loaf of bread and a bottle of wine. Cold quiche is also the perfect picnic item for a day spent touring the local wineries.

Crust

This is a basic pastry crust. Feel free to use whatever type of shortening you wish. Vegetable shortening is standard, but not local. Local butter will make for a richer crust. My mother saved bacon drippings (as do I), which I think make the best crust. If you cook local bacon and use locally milled flour you can create a Locavore pastry crust. For a 9-inch pie shell:

1 1/2 cups flour*   *1/4 teaspoon salt*
3–4 tablespoons ice water   *1/2 cup shortening, butter or bacon fat*

* For local flour use New Hope Mills or Birkett Mills pastry flour

In a mixing bowl combine salt and flour. Cut in shortening with pastry cutter or two knives until you have a coarse mixture with bits of shortening the size of small peas. This can also be done in a food processor by pulsing together a few times. Sprinkle a few tablespoons of water over the mixture and gently stir (or pulse together in a food processor). Add additional water until crust just holds together when pressed into a ball. Don't over-mix or over-process, to avoid making the pastry tough. Cover and lest rest under refrigeration for a few minutes.

Roll out on a floured surface and lay pastry into a pie plate. Prick surface of crust with fork. Bake 10 minutes in a 425°F oven.

Filling

There are innumerable combinations of fillings for quiche. That is what makes it a fun dish to make from local, in-season ingredients. The following version calls for bacon; however, ham, chicken, smoked sausage are all great choices. The recipe calls for Swiss cheese; ask your local cheese producer for their closest equivalent. Local mushrooms, spinach, onions, squash, eggplant can all be used. In all, you want about one cup total of filling between the meat and/or vegetables, plus the cheese and liquid.

4 eggs
1/4 teaspoon salt
dash cayenne pepper
1 cup shredded Swiss cheese
dash nutmeg
1/2 cup crisp bacon
1/2 cup sautéed mushrooms
2 cups half-and-half or light cream

Preheat over to 425°F. Scatter bacon and mushrooms over crust. Top with shredded cheese. In a bowl, beat eggs. Add cream, salt and spices and mix. Pour over cheese without overflowing the edge of the crust. Bake 15 minutes, the reduce heat to 350°F and bake an additional 30 minutes or until a knife in the center comes out clean. Remove from oven and let sit a few minutes to set. Cut into wedges and serve hot or cold.

Makes 6 servings.

Pork with Apple Onion Glaze
Recipe on page 98

Side Dishes

A great side dish can make a meal. They don't need to be complicated, just good. It's how they accent the main course that scores points.

Side dishes also add nutritional complements to the meal.

Potatoes

◁ OVEN FRIES ▷

Making real French fries at home is messy and inconvenient. Most of us don't keep a deep fryer set up. Besides, let's face it, fries are not the healthiest side dish in the world. Oven roasted fries are a great alternative. Quick to make, low in fat and full of flavor, they are a favorite at Allens Hill Farm. We enjoy them with any meal where French fries would be the choice.

3 russet potatoes
2 tablespoons vegetable oil
1/2 teaspoon seasoned salt
1/2 teaspoon black pepper

Preheat the oven to 450°F with a rack in the upper third of the oven. Scrub the potatoes. Dry with a paper towel. Cut each potato into half lengthwise. Cut each half lengthwise again, then each quarter in half again. This will yield eight wedges per potato. Place into a mixing bowl. Add oil and seasonings and toss. Place wedges onto a sheet pan, skin side down. Roast about 20 minutes or until the wedges begin to brown nicely and potatoes are soft inside.

Makes 4 servings.

Variations

◁ Sweet potato fries: For a more colorful and nutritious alternative, use sweet potatoes in place of regular potatoes.

◁ Cajun Fries: Before mixing, sprinkle potatoes liberally with Cajun seasoning.

◁ HERB ROASTED POTATOES ▷

These are similar to oven fries, but have a different shape and flavor. They go great with meats and poultry.

3 russet potatoes
1/2 teaspoon salt
1/2 teaspoon granulated garlic
2 tablespoons vegetable oil
1/2 teaspoon black pepper
1 tablespoon of fresh rosemary

Preheat the oven to 450°F with a rack in the upper third of the oven. Scrub the potatoes. Dry with a paper towel. Cut each potato into half lengthwise. Cut each half lengthwise again, then each quarter in half again. This will yield eight wedges per potato. Cut each wedge into four chunks.

Place potato chunks into a mixing bowl. Add oil and seasonings and toss. Place potatoes onto a sheet pan. Roast about 20 minutes or until the wedges begin to brown nicely.

Makes 4 servings.

Baked Potato

There is nothing like a great baked potato. There really is no substitute for a good russet potato. I think the skin is the treat at the end, so I want it to be crisp and tasty. Therefore, I lightly oil and salt my spuds.

kosher salt
non-stick cooking spray
4 russet potatoes, washed and scrubbed

Preheat the oven to 450°F.

Place the potatoes on a baking sheet. Spray lightly with non-stick cooking spray and sprinkle lightly with kosher salt. Bake for about 45 minutes or until soft when pierced with a knife.

Serve immediately with plenty of butter, sour cream, fresh ground pepper and freshly chopped chives.

Makes 4 servings.

Twice Baked Potato Casserole

This dish is a holiday tradition at Allens Hill Farm; rich, delicious and flavorful.

1/2 cup sour cream
1 tablespoon parsley
1/2 teaspoon pepper
1/4 cup milk or as needed
1 cup shredded cheddar cheese
4 green onions sliced
4 slices cooked bacon
1/4 cup melted butter
1/2 teaspoon seasoned salt
4 large baking potatoes (russets)

Bake potatoes in a 450°F oven until done, about an hour. (This can be done a day ahead). When potatoes are cool enough to handle, scoop out the insides into a mixing bowl. Cut up skins into one-inch pieces and add. Add remaining ingredients and stir until well combined. Add more milk if needed so that mixture just holds together. Pour into a greased casserole dish. Bake at 350°F until hot and top begins to brown.

Makes 4 to 6 servings.

Smashed Potatoes

This is a recipe which allows you to "just do it".

Start out with some boiled spuds. If you can get some Yukon golds, they work great for any boiled potato dish. Then add what you like. Make them as simple or as extravagant as you like. I'll provide some suggested ingredients. The only real trick is to make sure that you add the right amount of liquid to get the final consistency you desire.

1/2 cup or more milk	4 slices cooked bacon
1/4 cup melted butter	salt and pepper to taste
1 cup shredded cheddar cheese	1/2 cup of chopped green onion
4–6 potatoes depending on size	

Scrub and wash the spuds. Do not peel. Get a large pot and put in the potatoes either whole or if you want them too cook a bit faster, cut into quarters. Cover the potatoes with cold water. Add a teaspoon of salt to the water and set to boil. Cook until the spuds are cooked: soft when pierced with a fork. Drain the potatoes and put into a mixing bowl or leave in the pot.

Roughly mash or "smash" the potatoes. Add the remaining ingredients and combine. If the potatoes are too dry, add more milk. Try not to over-stir; remember you want "smashed" not mashed. Note: it's a good idea to warm the milk before adding to the potatoes so you don't reduce the serving temperature of the potatoes by adding cold milk.

Makes 4–6 servings.

Home Fries

Home Fries are not just for breakfast anymore. They go great with all kinds of meals. You'll find the recipe in the chapter on breakfast under the section on side dishes on page 46.

Rice

Rice is simple, versatile and economical. Just follow the directions on the package.

Why did I bother to even put it in this cookbook? Just to remind you to make rice once in a while. It goes with almost anything. I like it with chicken and seafood in particular.

Cook some extra and use the leftovers for fried rice.

For our Fried Rice recipe, see page 59.

Leftover rice can also be used in our Super Simple Soup recipe (see page 60).

Bread-Based Sides

STUFFING

This is a basic, all-purpose stuffing: good with chicken or pork. Feel free to add sausage, nuts, other seasonings, raisins, etc.

> 4 cups breadcrumbs
> 1/2 cup (1 stick) butter
> salt and pepper to taste
> 1 teaspoon rubbed sage
> 1 small onion, finely chopped
> 1/2 cup finely chopped celery

Put breadcrumbs into a mixing bowl.

Add butter to skillet. Sautee the onions and celery in the butter until soft. Pour into mixing bowl. Add salt and pepper to taste. Mix until well combined.

If stuffing seems dry, add a bit of water or chicken stock.

REAL GARLIC BREAD

My son loves garlic bread. It goes well with salads, Italian foods, beef, seafood…almost anything. It's easy to make and can perk up an otherwise boring meal.

My farm market stall always seems to be next to farmers who grow garlic. I've become a fan and student of garlic.

You can make garlic bread the way our mothers did with garlic powder, but it's best to use the real thing. Fresh garlic is just amazing.

There are so many different types of garlic it's impossible to get into a discussion here.

Take my advice. Locally grown garlic is vastly superior to most supermarket varieties. It is more flavorful and is more pungent. Buy a bunch and store in a cool, dry place—it will keep for months.

For a few weeks in the spring, you can find "green garlic." It is immature garlic that the farmers have pulled to thin out the field to allow the remaining garlic to grow larger. It is great. Use it like green onions or scallions. Chop up the white bulb and the green. It is just the best. If you see it, buy it. It's only available for a few weeks in the spring. It is outstanding for garlic bread.

dash of salt
1 teaspoon dried parsley flakes
1/2 cup softened butter or margarine
1 loaf fresh Italian or French bread
2-4 cloves fresh garlic depending on taste, peeled and minced

Preheat oven to 450°F. Put a rack in the top third of the oven.

Good bread is important for good garlic bread. Slice the bread about an inch thick. If using French bread, slice on a diagonal so the slice is four to five inches across. I would figure on at least two pieces per person.

You will need at least one tablespoon of butter for every two pieces of bread and one clove of garlic, minimum, per each tablespoon of butter. So if you have eight slices of garlic bread, you will need 4 tablespoons of butter and 4 cloves of garlic.

Mix butter and minced garlic together in a small bowl along with a dash of salt and a teaspoon of parsley flakes for some color. If you like your garlic bread real buttery and garlicky (like me), feel free to make more garlic butter and spread it on thick.

Spread garlic butter on one side of the bread and put the slices buttered side up on a baking sheet. Toast in oven for 5–10 minutes.

When the pieces just begin to brown, it's done.

Makes 6 to 8 servings.

Variation

Garlic Cheese Bread: Feel free to sprinkle with grated parmesan cheese or shredded mozzarella before baking.

The Allens Hill Farm Cookbook

vegetables

It's extremely important to make sure supper is a well balanced meal. This means at least one, preferably two vegetables with your entrée unless vegetables are a major component of the meal. Of course, fresh vegetables are always preferable. However, out of season, these may be cost prohibitive. Frozen vegetables are fine. The quality is good and they are quite economical. Just rip open the bag and follow the directions

In season, get to your local farmer's market. The quality, freshness, variety and value are unbeatable. I'll offer a couple of suggestions for some fresh vegetable sides. Experiment! Be bold! Better yet, plant a garden yourself and enjoy unltimate freshness.

It is very important to get your kids to buy into vegetables at an early age. Get them involved by showing them how to pick them out at the market, how to clean, prepare and enjoy. Once they discover purple carrots and orange cauliflower, veggies just become more fun.

~ Crudités ~

Crudités is the fancy name for raw vegetables. Some kids are not big on cooked vegetables, but will chow on carrot and celery sticks. Mushrooms, green peppers, sugar snap pea pods, radishes, green onions, cucumbers, broccoli, cauliflower are all good choices. This is another way to take advantage of farmer's market abundance. Some non-fat dip or dressing can also entice the consumption of more vegetables. This is a great alternative to chips.

Zucchini

For any of you who have grown zucchini, you know it is incredibly prolific. Therefore, it tends to be readily available and reasonably priced. It lends itself to many preparations and makes a colorful addition to a meal. I prefer small to medium sized zucchini. Avoid those that are the size of baseball bats. In addition to the traditional green, farmers are now growing yellow zucchini which make a nice looking presentation when you mix the two.

Sautéed

Wash and slice the zucchini about one-quarter-inch thick. If the slices are over one-and-a-half inches in diameter, cut them in half. Place a skillet over medium high heat. When hot, add some olive oil and the zucchini. If you like onions, add a few thinly sliced onions. Stir frequently until the zucchini is just heated through. It should be hot, but still have some crunch. This goes well with lighter dishes like chicken or fish.

Grilled

For this recipe, a little bit larger squash is better. Wash the zucchini. Slice on an angle so that the slice is about three inches across and three-eighths inch thick. You can do this on an outdoor grill or a grill pan on the stove. Spray the slices with butter flavored non-stick cooking spray and sprinkle with grill seasoning. Place on medium hot grill and cook until al dente. If they are browning too quickly, move to a cooler part of the grill. These are great with grilled chicken or seafood and as a garnish for a dinner salad.

Marinara

Preheat the oven to 350°F. Wash and slice the zucchini to fill a casserole dish about two-thirds full. Add pasta sauce, about one-half cup of grated parmesan cheese and a sprinkle of oregano and stir. Use enough sauce to generously cover the slices. Place in the oven and cook until zucchini is just tender.

Winter Squash
with Allens Hill Farm Apple Cider Molasses

4 tablespoons butter
salt and pepper if desired
Allens Hill Farm Apple Cider Molasses
2 small winter squash such as acorn, delicate, or carnivale

Preheat oven to 400°F. Cut squash in half and clean out seeds. Place on baking sheet. In the cavity, place a tablespoon of butter, lightly salt and pepper if desired and drizzle apple cider molasses over the top. Bake for an hour or until the flesh is tender.

Bacon Wrapped Green Beans

This is an elegant side. Steam fresh green beans until just tender. Make each portion into a bundle and wrap in a cooked bacon strip.

Don't overcook the bacon, or you won't be able to wrap it around the beans.

Mushrooms

Sautéed mushrooms are an excellent complement to beef dishes of all kinds. They also go well with poultry and seafood. Throw some on top of a burger. They are quick and easy to prepare.

Wash and slice as many or few mushrooms as you like. A half-pound makes a good sized portion. Put a skillet on medium heat. Add a couple of tablespoons of butter, melt, and add the mushrooms. Add a clove or two of minced garlic if you like. Fresh ground pepper or salt is good as well. When the mushrooms begin to soften and give up their moisture, you can also add a splash of white wine. Cook until the moisture is not quite gone.

Corn

Is there anything better than fresh sweet corn during the summer? Buy it while you can. The good news is that many farmers are using different varieties and farming practices which have extended the season dramatically. The latest varieties of super sweet corn, which most farmers are using, practically assure your corn is going to be sweet, and delicious. My advice is to find a farm stand or farm market vendor whose corn you really like and stick with them.

Perhaps the worst sin in cooking corn is to overcook it. Once the corn is thoroughly heated, it's done. Our mothers boiled it to death. Newer varieties require less cooking.

There are several methods to cook sweet corn on the cob.

When I'm making a quick supper, I like to steam it. Just put the husked corn into the steaming pot and cook 5-7 minutes. It you don't have a steamer, I suggest using just a small amount of water in the bottom of a large covered pot.

You can boil the corn in a large pot of water, but boiled corn loses some of its flavor and nutrients during the cooking process.

The most flavorful way to cook sweet corn is to roast it on the grill. Soak the corn, husks and all for at least an hour. Place on the grill and roast, turning frequently, until the corn begins to feel a bit tender when you press on the outside, or carefully open the top of an ear and check for doneness. Remove from the grill. Using gloves, husk the corn and serve.

BE CAREFUL WHEN REMOVING THE HUSKS—IT'S HOT.

Husked corn can also be cooked directly on the grill. Simply spray the ears lightly with non-stick cooking spray and place on a medium hot grill. Turn frequently. The corn takes only a few minutes to cook.

Grilled Tomatoes with Dukkah

olive oil
salt and pepper
2 fresh firm tomatoes
Allens Hill Farm Dukkah Hazzard or Down Under Dukkah

Choose ripe firm tomatoes. Wash and remove stem. Cut in half and brush with oil. Sprinkle lightly with salt and pepper. Grill or broil the cut side until lightly carmelized. Plate and sprinkle with dukkah.

Makes 4 servings.

Twice-Baked Potato Casserole
Recipe on page 105

Salad Greens

One of the biggest reasons we can't get our kids to eat more greens is that we have been in the habit of serving tasteless iceberg lettuce as the standard salad lettuce. Growing up, we always had salad greens from the garden during the summer. Lettuce is so easy to grow. I recommend it to anyone who has the space. Even a flower bed is big enough to grow a lot of lettuce. You can't beat the freshness and flavor.

My farmer's market experience has taught me that there are a lot of great salad greens available. Many farms sell bags of mixed greens. These are full of wonderful, contrasting flavors and look great on a plate. Some farms even grow these hydroponically (using water instead of soil), so they are available year round.

Your best resource is the farmer you buy from. You should be able to taste a leaf and have the farmer explain the differences between the varieties as well as suggestions on how to use them. These greens may be a bit more expensive than a head of iceberg, but they are certainly competitively priced with the bagged salad mixes in your supermarket. Once you try good salad greens, you (and your kids) will be hooked.

You still need a dressing to bring it all together. Any store bought dressing you like is just fine, but try the French Apple Dressing in the Pantry Checklist section on page 176. When making a salad, keep a couple of things in mind. A wonderfully healthy and low calorie salad can be destroyed with rich dressing. Think about a low fat or fat free dressing if you are concerned about calories.

It's also about how much dressing you use. Less is more. Use half of your normal amount of dressing and thoroughly toss the dressing to completely coat the salad. You'll find that the flavor is better with much less dressing, it's healthier and you'll save a lot of money on dressing.

Beans

ALLENS HILL FARM BAKED BEANS

2 teaspoons salt
1 pound Navy beans
salt and pepper to taste
1 teaspoon dry mustard
1/2 pound bacon or salt pork
1/2 cup Allens Hill Farm Apple Cider Molasses

Put beans into a bowl. Rinse with cold water and check for debris. Cover with fresh water and soak overnight. The next day, drain water and put beans into a pot. Cover with cold water. Add two teaspoons salt and bring to a boil. Skim if necessary, cover loosely and cook 30–40 minutes until beans are just tender; don't overcook. Drain beans and set aside.

While beans are cooking get your bean pot or covered casserole. Cut up bacon or salt pork into half-inch cubes and put into bottom of pot. In a separate pot, bring a few quarts of water to a boil. Preheat oven to 300°F.

Put cooked and drain beans into pot with bacon. Add molasses, mustard, salt and pepper to taste and stir. Add boiling water to cover beans. Cover and put into oven. Bake about 4 hours until beans are tender.

Raise temperature to 400°F. Remove pot, uncover and stir. Put back in oven, stirring every ten minutes until desired degree of browning is reached.

Makes 4 to 6 servings.

Variation

Vegan Beans: Omit meat and prepare as above. To keep a smoky flavor, reduce apple cider molasses to one-quarter cup and add one-quarter cup of Allens Hill Farm Smokey Apple Glaze. For a spiced flavor use Allens Hill Farm Spiced Apple Glaze.

A Change of Pace

APPLESAUCE

Applesauce is so easy to make, why buy it?

The key to great applesauce is using a mixture of apples. Make sure some are tart, cooking apples. I love Cortlands in my applesauce.

There really are no proportions for this recipe. If you make lots of applesauce, spring for an apple peeler. For a small investment, you can peel apples in seconds.

sugar, cinnamon and nutmeg (optional)
apples peeled, cored and cut into chunks

Put the apples into a heavy saucepan or stockpot. Add a little bit of water to cover the bottom of the pan to avoid scorching. Cover pan and put on medium low heat. Stir occasionally.

When the chunks begin to break apart, watch apples closely. When all the pieces are softened, stir to break them apart. Remove from the heat. This will result in a nicely textured, not too smooth applesauce.

When it cools a bit, taste.

The type of apples you have used will determine how tart your applesauce is. If it's too tart, add just a bit of sugar. I add just a teaspoon or two at a time until the tartness is in balance. I like to add just a dash of cinnamon and nutmeg. However, if you like cinnamon in your applesauce, add as much as you like.

Applesauce also freezes well.

Fresh Baked Goodies and Dessert Treats

THE ALLENS HILL FARM COOKBOOK

Breakfast Baked Goods

Breakfast baked goods are my greatest weakness. I'll take a dozen fresh doughnuts over a filet mignon any day. There is something immensely satisfying about a fresh doughnut, coffee cake or muffin. They just seem to be the ideal companion to a tall, ice cold glass of milk or steaming cup of fresh brewed coffee or tea. Yes, these items can be a bit hard on the waistline, but in moderation, they are pure joy.

Breakfast Breads
see following pages for recipes

Cinnamon Buns

◥ MIKE'S FAVORITE CINNAMON BUNS ◤

One of our holiday traditions is to make a big pan of cinnamon buns for breakfast. We never seem to get to the bacon and eggs since we gorge ourselves on these luscious rolls. Sweet, soft dough rolled around plump raisins, cinnamon and sugar and enveloped by vanilla icing make these simply irresistible. I can't vouch for how fresh they will be the next day; they never seem to make it past lunchtime. The best part is, these can be prepared the night before and baked fresh in the morning. You won't need alarm clocks in the house when the fragrant aroma of fresh baked cinnamon buns wafts through the house. My son Mike requests these every holiday.

This is a great recipe to get the kids involved since it is a special treat. Show them the ingredients and how to properly measure them. If mixing by hand let them take a turn stirring. If using an electric mixer, explain safety and how to operate if they are old enough. Kneading dough by hand is great fun for kids and they can't do it any harm. Kids are fascinated by rising dough; it's cool to them. They can help roll it out. Brushing on the butter and putting on the fillings is perfect for a smaller child. Every kid loves the last part: spreading on the icing. However, don't neglect one of the most fundamental lessons: clean up after yourself. Cooking is fun, but the dishes must also be done and the counters wiped.

Dough
2 cups milk   1 cup sugar
2 teaspoons salt   1/2 cup warm water
1/2 cup (1 stick) butter   6–7 cups all-purpose flour
2 tablespoons yeast (or 2 packages)

Filling
1 cup sugar   2 cups raisins
6 tablespoons butter   1 tablespoon cinnamon

Icing
1 teaspoon vanilla
4–5 tablespoons milk
2 cups confectioners sugar

Scald milk in a saucepan (see note below on scalding milk). Add butter, sugar and salt. Cool to lukewarm.

In a large bowl or mixer bowl, dissolve yeast in lukewarm water with a dash of sugar. Yeast should be bubbly after a few minutes. Add milk mixture and beat in flour until dough forms.

Knead either by hand or machine until the dough is smooth and elastic, adding more flour as needed. Put dough in a greased bowl, cover and let rise in a warm place until double in bulk.

While dough is rising, prepare filling. Put raisins in a bowl and cover with hot water to plump them. Melt butter. Mix together sugar and cinnamon.

Flour a large work surface. Put raised dough on surface and roll into a rectangle 24 inches long by 12 inches wide. Drain raisins. Brush melted butter over surface of the dough. Sprinkle cinnamon sugar and scatter raisins over dough. Roll up dough so that you have a 24-inch-long cylinder. Pinch the edge of the dough into the side of the roll to keep it in place and put seam side down. Slice with a sharp knife into 24 one-inch rolls (it's perfectly acceptable to use a ruler).

Now you have a few options. If you plan to bake the entire batch, place rolls into two greased 13x9-inch pans or a larger pan. You may also freeze the buns at this time to use at a later date.

If you are baking the buns today, preheat your oven to 425°F, cover the buns and let rise until double in bulk.

If you want to bake the next day, cover pan and refrigerate. Take the buns out the next day, start your oven and let buns rise until double.

Bake 13–18 minutes until done. Buns should be lightly brown and have an internal temp of 200°F. Turn onto rack to cool.

Mix icing ingredients together, adding enough milk to achieve desired consistency. While buns are still slightly warm, spread icing over the buns.

Eat immediately!

Makes 2 dozen.

Note on Scalding Milk

For the dough to behave properly, milk needs to be scalded to the proper temperature. Tests indicate that one minute at 198°F. or seven minutes at 185°F. will alter the milk proteins so that they will react properly with the flour proteins to produce a quality dough. Failure to heat the milk sufficiently may cause the dough to be "slack".

Coffee Cakes

There are countless styles of coffee cakes. I prefer those made without yeast. Moist, sweet and dense, the flavor and texture actually improve as the cake mellows overnight. The following are two of my favorites. If you want to add to the presentation, and calories, by all means drizzle a thin stream of icing over any of the following.

Quick Crumb Coffee Cake

This is a quick coffee cake. If there isn't time the night before, you can whip it up in just a few minutes and finish making breakfast while it's baking (though this cake will be moister the following day). For this version I like to put all of the streusel on top, but feel free to layer half in the batter and put the rest on top. Either way is just fine.

Batter

2 eggs
1-1/3 cup milk
2 teaspoons vanilla
2-1/2 cups all-purpose flour
1 cup sugar
1/2 teaspoon salt
1/2 cup (1 stick butter)
4 teaspoons baking powder

Topping

2/3 cup sugar
1 teaspoon cinnamon
1/4 cup melted butter
1/4 cup all-purpose flour

Preheat oven to 375°F. Prepare the topping. Stir together dry ingredients. Stir melted butter into dry mix with fork and stir until crumbly. Set aside.

Prepare batter. Mix together flour, salt and baking powder. Beat butter and sugar until light. Beat in eggs one at a time until incorporated. Alternately add dry ingredients and milk (four parts dry to three parts milk), stirring between each addition until mixed. When complete stir in vanilla. Pour batter into a greased 13x9-inch pan. Scatter topping over batter. Bake 25–30 minutes or until a toothpick inserted in center comes out clean.

Optional: mix one cup of confectioner's sugar with about three teaspoons of milk to make a pourable icing. Drizzle a thin stream of icing over the cooled cake.

Makes about 20 pieces.

Variation

Individual Crumb Cakes: Prepare topping and batter as above. Preheat over to 400°F. Fill muffin tins two-thirds full of batter and sprinkle on topping mixture. Bake about 20 minutes or until done.

This is great kid fun. Let them fill the muffin tins. Since this can be messy, it provides excellent finger licking opportunities. Mixing together the crumb topping is a good kid job.

Makes about 2 dozen.

Sour Cream Coffee Cake

This coffee cake recipe comes direct from Mom. The sour cream makes it rich and moist. Nuts are optional, but a good choice. Be sure to put a layer of the topping mix in the center.

Batter

2 eggs	1 cup sugar
1 cup sour cream	1 teaspoon vanilla
2 cups all-purpose flour	1/2 cup (1 stick) butter
1 teaspoon baking soda	1 tablespoon lemon juice
1 teaspoon baking powder	

Topping/Filling

1/2 cup chopped walnuts
1/2 cup brown sugar
1 teaspoon cinnamon

Preheat oven to 375°F.

Prepare topping by mixing ingredients together.

Prepare batter. Beat butter and sugar together until light. Beat in eggs, and then add lemon juice and vanilla. Mix together remaining dry ingredients and add to butter mixture. Mix well.

Grease a 13x9-inch pan. Put in half of the batter. Sprinkle two-thirds of the filling over the batter then layer remaining batter over the top. Sprinkle with the rest of the topping mix.

Bake 30 minutes or until a toothpick inserted in the center comes out clean.

Makes about 20 pieces.

Kuchen

Kuchen is a yeasted breakfast cake. In my mother's German family it was a traditional Sunday breakfast treat. The dough is less sweet and dense than coffee cake. It is the toppings that give a basic Kuchen its distinctiveness. I offer a few suggestions, but feel free to use your imagination. I am partial to the peanut & coconut myself. As with the coffee cakes, feel free to drizzle glaze over these. Kids can be involved in the whole process of making Kuchen. They especially enjoy putting on the various toppings.

Dough

1 egg	1 cup milk
1/3 cup sugar	1 teaspoon salt
1 tablespoon yeast	1/2 cup warm water
4 cups all-purpose flour	1/4 cup (1/2 stick) butter

Egg wash
beat 1 egg with a dash of salt

Scald milk (see note page 120). Add butter, sugar and salt. Pour into mixing bowl and let cool to lukewarm. Dissolve yeast in warm water with a pinch of sugar. When foamy, add to milk mixture. Beat in egg and flour. Mix until dough forms. Knead until dough is smooth and elastic, adding flour as necessary. Put into greased bowl, cover and let rise until triple in bulk. Grease three round cake pans. Punch down dough and divide into three equal parts. Roll out to about a half-inch thick and put into pans. Brush with egg wash and add toppings. Preheat oven to 400°F. Let rise until double in bulk. Bake about 15–20 minutes until done. Remove from pan and cool on rack.

Option: Roll out dough one-half-inch thick. Cut with a three-inch biscuit cutter to make individual Kuchen. Place on baking sheets. Proceed as above. Reduce baking time by about 5 minutes.

Toppings

Streusel: Mix together one-quarter cup of flour, one-quarter cup of sugar, one-half teaspoon cinnamon and a dash of salt. Add one-and-a-half tablespoons of melted butter. Stir with fork until crumbly. Scatter over dough.

Peanut: Chop one-half cup of peanuts and scatter over dough.

Coconut: Scatter shredded coconut over dough.

Peanut and Coconut: Scatter equal portion of chopped peanut and coconut over dough.

Apple: Peel and thinly slice 1-2 apples and layer over dough. Sprinkle with sugar or cinnamon sugar.

Cinnamon Sugar: Stir one-half teaspoon of cinnamon into one-quarter cup of sugar and sprinkle over dough.

Makes about 24 pieces.

 # Muffins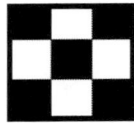

There are literally millions of muffin recipes. Many of us only know the modern muffin which seems to about half the size of a birthday cake. The following recipes are for the standard home muffin tin. Muffins allow for great creativity. They can be savory as well as sweet. Take advantage of seasonal fruits. Muffin batter can be prepared the night before and then baked fresh in the morning.

Muffin Pointers

Cookbooks have been devoted exclusively to muffins. I cannot begin to do anything but touch upon some of the basics and a few popular recipes. Still, there are a few tips which will help you to create and adapt recipes to develop your own favorite.

Muffins are leavened in one of two ways; with baking powder or a combination of baking powder and baking soda. Baking soda is used when acidic ingredients are used in the recipe such as buttermilk or molasses. A rough rule of thumb would be to decrease baking powder by two teaspoons and add one-half teaspoon of soda for each cup of an acidic ingredient. You can see this in the difference between the basic muffin recipe and the buttermilk muffin recipe below.

The amount of leavening must be adjusted when additional ingredients are added. In an average muffin recipe with two cups of flour, adding a cup of fruit would warrant the addition of an extra teaspoon of baking powder.

When baking muffins with molasses or honey, reduce the baking temperature. The muffins will tend to darken if baked at the usual temperatures of 400°F, so try 350°F or even 325°F and cook longer until done.

Almost any quick bread recipe can be made as a muffin. So if you have a favorite banana or zucchini bread recipe, try it as a muffin.

One cup of fresh buttermilk may be replaced with one-quarter cup of dried buttermilk and one cup of water. Simply mix the buttermilk into the dry ingredients and add water in place of buttermilk. This works very well and is a great way to avoid waste while you make sure that you have buttermilk available when you need it.

Most muffin recipes call for a minimal amount of mixing. Just a quick stir will do; a few lumps are fine. Over-mixing promotes gluten development and a tough muffin.

Muffins can be spruced up with a variety of toppings. Coarse sugar is very easy and attractive. Cinnamon sugar is great as well. Streusel is also excellent (see recipe for Kuchen toppings on page 123).

Muffins are the ideal kid friendly recipe. They can easily complete the recipe from start to finish. Just provide some guidance and let them have at it! If they are younger, help with the oven. Also make sure they clean up after themselves.

Simple Muffins

These are the starting point. These are as basic as muffins get.

2 eggs 1 cup milk
1/2 cup sugar 1/2 teaspoon salt
2 cups all-purpose flour 1 tablespoon baking powder
1/4 cup vegetable oil or melted butter

Preheat oven to 400°F.

Mix dry ingredients together. Add remaining ingredients and stir until just mixed. Spoon into prepared muffin tins about two-thirds full.

Bake 15–20 minutes until done.

Makes 12 muffins.

Simple Buttermilk Muffins

These are the county cousins of the simple muffins above. Note the difference in the leavenings.

- 2 eggs
- 1 cup buttermilk
- 2 cups all-purpose flour
- 1/2 teaspoon baking soda
- 1/2 cup sugar
- 1/2 teaspoon salt
- 1 teaspoon baking powder
- 1/4 cup vegetable oil or melted butter

Preheat oven to 400°F. Mix dry ingredients together. Add remaining ingredients and stir until just mixed. Spoon into prepared muffin tins about two-thirds full. Bake 15–20 minutes until done.

Makes 12 muffins.

Variations

Use either of the two recipes above as the basis for the following variations.

Berry: add one teaspoon of baking powder to the dry ingredients. Stir a cup of fresh berries, blueberries, blackberries, raspberries, etc, into the batter.

Apple: add one-and-a-half teaspoons of baking powder, one-half teaspoon of cinnamon, one-quarter teaspoon of nutmeg and one-quarter cup of sugar to the dry ingredients. Peel and chop one cup of apples. Stir into the batter. Great with streusel topping.

Chocolate Chip: add one teaspoon of baking powder to dry ingredients. Stir one cup of chocolate chips into batter. Sprinkle with coarse sugar.

Chocolate Chocolate Chip: add one-half teaspoon baking powder, one-half teaspoon baking soda and one-third cup of cocoa powder to the dry mix. Stir one cup of chocolate chips to the batter.

Dried Fruit: soak one-half cup of dried raisins, cranberries, dates, or any dried fruit in hot water to cover. Add one teaspoon of baking powder to the dry mix. Drain fruit. Stir into the batter.

Buttermilk Muffins with Crumb Topping

These are basic buttermilk muffins with a twist. A portion of the muffin mixture is set aside to use as a crumb topping. These muffins have the wonderful old fashioned combination of cinnamon and nutmeg flavor.

- 1 cup buttermilk
- 2 large eggs, beaten
- 1/2 teaspoon cinnamon
- 2-1/2 cups all-purpose flour
- 1/2 teaspoon salt
- 1/4 teaspoon nutmeg
- 1/2 teaspoon baking soda
- 2 teaspoons baking powder
- 2 cups lightly packed light brown sugar
- 2/3 cup vegetable shortening or butter

Preheat oven to 400°F.

Mix flour, sugar, salt and spices together. Cut in vegetable shortening until the mixture looks like coarse bread crumbs. Reserve a half-cup of this mixture. Add baking powder and soda. Stir to mix. Then add buttermilk and eggs. Stir until well blended.

Spoon batter into prepared muffin pans, (either lined with muffin papers or greased) until the cups are about two-thirds full. Sprinkle on reserved crumb topping.

Bake 15–20 minutes or until a toothpick inserted in the center comes out clean. Remove from muffin tins. Serve warm.

Makes 12 muffins.

Allens Hill Farm Corn Muffins

This recipe uses Allens Hill Farm's signature product, Apple Cider Molasses. This all natural sweetener made from pure apple cider gives these muffins a distinctive flavor and color. This is a food you might have eaten 200 years ago. See the supplier list in the back of the book for information on where to obtain it. If you can't find our Apple Cider Molasses, substitute sugar or honey.

```
        1 egg            1 cup milk
    3/4 cup cornmeal     1 cup all-purpose flour
 1 teaspoon baking soda  2 teaspoons baking powder
    2 tablespoons oil or melted butter (optional)
    1/4 cup Allens Hill Farm Apple Cider Molasses
```

Preheat oven to 375°F.

Mix dry ingredients together. Add remaining ingredients and stir until just moistened. Spoon in to prepared muffin tins about two-thirds full. Bake 20–25 minutes until a toothpick inserted in the center comes out clean.

Makes 12 muffins.

Bran Muffins

Can you say fiber??

```
        1 egg              1 cup milk
    1/4 cup sugar          1/2 teaspoon salt
  1 cup all bran cereal    1 cup all-purpose flour
 1 tablespoon baking powder  2 tablespoons melted butter
```

Preheat oven to 375°F. Stir together milk and bran cereal and let stand for ten minutes. Mix dry ingredients together. Add egg and butter to cereal mixture. Stir dry into wet until just mixed. Spoon batter into prepared muffin pans about two-thirds full. Bake 15–20 minutes or until a toothpick inserted in to the center comes out clean.

Makes 12 muffins.

Oatmeal Muffins

This is a great way to use up leftover oatmeal cereal.

1 egg	1/2 cup milk
1/2 teaspoon salt	2 tablespoons sugar
1 cup cooked oatmeal	1/2 teaspoon cinnamon
1-1/2 cup all-purpose flour	4 teaspoons baking powder
2 tablespoons melted butter	

Preheat oven to 400°F. Mix dry ingredients together. Stir together remaining ingredients until well mixed. Stir in dry ingredients until just mixed. Spoon into prepared muffin tins about two-thirds full. Bake 15–20 minutes until a toothpick inserted in center comes out clean.

Makes 12 muffins.

Applesauce Muffins

These muffins are wonderfully moist and with a texture more like a cake than a muffin. Homemade applesauce makes a real difference if you have some. See the recipe on page 116. To add a twist, Allens Hill Farm Apple Cider Molasses makes these especially moist and flavorful.

1 egg	1 cup flour
1/3 cup raisins	1/4 cup sugar
1/4 teaspoon salt	1/2 cup applesauce
1/8 teaspoon cloves	1/2 teaspoon nutmeg
1 teaspoon baking soda	1/4 cup butter (1/2 stick)
1/3 cup chopped walnuts	1-1/2 teaspoons cinnamon
1/4 cup Allens Hill Farm Apple Cider Molasses	

Preheat oven to 350°F. Mix together flour, baking soda and spices, set aside. Cream butter, sugar and Apple Cider Molasses. Add egg and beat well. Add dry ingredients and mix. Add applesauce and mix until moist. Stir in raisins and walnuts. Spoon into prepared muffin tins about two-thirds full. Bake 25–30 minutes until done.

Makes 12 muffins.

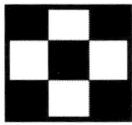 ## Scones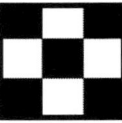

Scones are one of those things that sound like they should be complicated. Nothing could be further from the truth. There is a certain charm to a freshly baked scone. Though these recipes are included in the breakfast section, scones are perfectly acceptable to serve at almost any meal or in between since there are so many variations on the basic scone.

There are many options in shaping scones. The original shape of this traditional Scottish bread was a simple round flat loaf called a bannock or bannock bread. These were originally baked on a griddle, not in an oven.

The more common shape we see is wedge shaped. The scone dough is rolled or patted into a circle eight or nine inches in diameter, then cut into eight individual wedges. There are variations here as well. For a full sized scone, roll the dough about three-quarter-inch thick. For a scone better suited to a snack than as a main breakfast item, divide the dough in half. Roll about half inch thick and five to six inches in diameter. Cut as above into eight wedges. Scones can also be cut out using a biscuit or decorative cookie cutter.

The key to good scones is to remember: less is more. This is a simple food requiring very little effort. Don't overdo the mixing or you will get a tough scone.

Basic Scone

This recipe is a bit richer and sweeter than the most basic scone. Feel free to reduce the amount of butter and sugar. I also use an egg since I like what it does to the texture and flavor for a breakfast item. Feel free to leave it out; just add an extra quarter-cup of liquid if you do.

1 egg
1 cup buttermilk
3 cups all-purpose flour
1/2 cup (1 stick) cold butter
1/2 cup sugar
1/2 teaspoon salt
1/2 teaspoon baking soda
1 tablespoon baking powder

Preheat oven to 450°F.

Mix dry ingredients together in a large bowl. Cut butter into pieces, add to dry ingredients. Using a pastry blender, cut butter into flour until the butter is in small but discrete pieces, like breadcrumbs. Add buttermilk and stir just enough to moisten (about 20 quick strokes). Dump onto a floured work surface and gently knead about ten times, adding extra four as needed. Remember, less is more. Pat into a 9-inch circle. Using a knife or dough scraper cut into eight wedges. Cut straight down; don't saw. Place on an un-greased baking sheet. If you like, brush the tops with milk and sprinkle with sugar. Bake 15–20 minutes or just until they start to brown.

Makes 8 scones.

Variations

Cinnamon Raisin Scones: add one teaspoon cinnamon, one-and-a-half teaspoons baking powder to dry mixture. After cutting in the butter, add one cup of raisins. I like to drizzle the baked scones with a glaze made from one cup confectioner's sugar and two or three tablespoons of milk.

Apple Cinnamon Scones: add two teaspoons cinnamon, one-and-a-half teaspoons baking powder to dry mix. After cutting in the butter add one cup chopped apples. Glaze is pretty good on these also.

Pick Your Fruit: use just about any type of fruit you like, blueberries, cranberries, etc. Just prepare as the variation above using a cup of your favorite fruit. Add whatever spices you like.

Filled Scones: prepare one batch of basic scone dough. Divide in halves. Roll each half into eight-inch circles. Spread your favorite jam or one of the Danish fillings from page 123 on one circle. Place other circle on top. Cut and bake as above.

Oatmeal Raisin Scone

Imagine a big, soft oatmeal cookie.

1 cup milk	1 teaspoon salt
1-1/2 cups raisins	1/3 cup brown sugar
1-1/2 cups rolled oats	1 teaspoon cinnamon
1 tablespoon baking powder	1-1/2 cups all-purpose flour
1/2 cup (1 stick) cold butter	

Preheat oven to 450°F. Mix dry ingredients (except raisins) together in a large bowl. Cut butter into pieces and add to dry mix. Use a pastry blender to cut the butter into the dry mix until it is the consistency of breadcrumbs. Stir in raisins. Add milk and stir just enough to moisten, about 20 quick strokes. Turn onto floured work surface and gently knead about ten times. Divide dough into thirds and pat each part into circle about five inches in diameter. Quarter each circle. Place the 12 scones on an ungreased baking sheet. Brush the tops with milk and sprinkle with sugar. Bake 12–15 minutes until lightly brown.

Makes 12 scones.

 # English Muffins

If you have ever had a fresh, homemade English muffin, you never look at the store bought version quite the same again. There is no comparison in flavor or texture.

Homemade English Muffins are not difficult to make and are interesting in that they are bread baked on griddle.

ENGLISH MUFFINS

1 cup milk
2 teaspoons salt
1 tablespoon sugar
1/2 cup warm water
1 tablespoon dry yeast
3 cups all-purpose flour
4 tablespoons (1/2 stick) butter

Scald milk (see note page 120).

Stir in sugar, salt and butter. Let cool to lukewarm.

Add warm water and yeast to a mixing bowl with a dash of sugar. Whisk together. When yeast is foamy, add the milk mixture. Beat two cups of flour into the liquid. Cover and let rise until double in bulk. Stir in the remaining flour, cover and let rise until double again.

Turn dough onto a floured work surface and pat the dough until it is one-half-inch thick. Cut into circles using a three- or four-inch biscuit cutter. Put onto a cornmeal dusted pan. Cover and let rise until about double in bulk.

Grease and heat a griddle. Cook muffins at medium low heat about 7–8 minutes per side. Cool on rack.

Use a fork, not a knife, to split muffins prior to toasting.

Makes about 18 muffins.

Biscuits

Biscuits are not traditional breakfast fare for a Yankee like me. Until I lived south of the Mason-Dixon line, I never knew about biscuits and gravy for breakfast. Breakfast biscuits are a true Southern tradition.

As one may expect, there are countless biscuit recipes and techniques. Making the best biscuits has been an unending source of argument, competition and debate for centuries.

~ BUTTERMILK BISCUITS ~

I do not claim that my biscuits are the best ever, though they are pretty good: a basic buttermilk biscuit. This recipe uses buttermilk powder since it is easier to have available in the pantry than running out to buy fresh, but fresh is certainly acceptable.

> 1/2 teaspoon salt
> 1/2 teaspoon baking soda
> 2-1/2 cups all-purpose flour
> 1 tablespoon baking powder
> 1/2 cup cold butter or vegetable shortening
>
> 1 cup buttermilk, or
> 1/4 cup buttermilk powder and 1 cup cold water

Preheat oven to 425°F.

Mix all dry ingredients (including buttermilk powder, if used) in a large mixing bowl. Use a pastry cutter to cut the shortening into the mix until it is the size of small peas. Don't over blend. It is the discreet pieces of shortening that make the biscuits tender and flaky. Add the liquid and mix just until the dough comes together. Turn onto a floured work surface and gently knead five or six times until the dough has come together. Less is more. Pat the dough to one-half-inch thick. Cut with a biscuit cutter. Place biscuits on a baking sheet and bake 12–15 minutes until they are light golden brown. Remove from oven and brush the tops with melted butter if desired. Serve warm.

Makes about 12 biscuits.

Baking Powder Biscuits

Here is a traditional southern biscuit using self-rising flour. If you can't find self-rising flour in your part of the country, I have included a recipe to mix some up yourself. It's a snap to make. These are great southern biscuits, tender and flaky.

Note: these biscuits may be made the night before, covered loosely and stored in the refrigerator to be ready to pop in the oven the next morning.

Self Rising Flour
3 cups all-purpose flour
1-1/4 teaspoons salt
2 tablespoons baking powder

Place flour ingredients in a bowl and mix thoroughly with a wire whisk.

1 cup milk
1 tablespoon baking powder
1 tablespoon sugar
1 cup vegetable shortening
About 3 cups self rising flour

Preheat oven to 400°F.

Mix two cups of the flour, sugar and baking powder in a large mixing bowl. Use a pastry cutter to cut the shortening into the mix until it is the size of small peas. Don't over blend. It is the discreet pieces of shortening that make the biscuits tender and flaky. Add the milk and mix just until the dough comes together. Turn onto a floured work surface and gently knead five or six times by folding the dough over itself and patting gently. Add flour as needed to keep it from sticking. When the dough is smooth, gently pat the dough to three-quarters of an inch thick. Cut with a biscuit cutter. Place biscuits on a baking sheet and bake 15–20 minutes until they are light golden brown. Remove from oven and brush the tops with melted butter if desired. Serve warm.

Makes about 12 biscuits.

Cinnamon Raisin Biscuits

Though die-hard southerners would probably turn in their grave, I think these biscuits are great. It's almost as good as a true cinnamon bun, and has the merits of being much quicker to make. These were inspired by the great cinnamon raisin biscuits my wife and I used to get at a favorite restaurant when we lived in Virginia.

1 cup raisins
1/2 teaspoon salt
1/2 cup (1 stick) butter
4 teaspoons baking powder
1 cup buttermilk
1 teaspoon cinnamon
1/2 teaspoon baking soda
2-1/4 cups all-purpose flour

Glaze
2–3 teaspoons milk
1 cup confectioner's sugar

Preheat oven to 425°F.

Mix together flour, salt, baking powder and soda in a large mixing bowl. Use a pastry cutter to cut the shortening into the mix until it is the size of small peas. Don't over blend. It is the discreet pieces of shortening that make the biscuits tender and flaky. Add the buttermilk and mix just until the dough comes together. Turn onto a floured work surface. Sprinkle the cinnamon and raisins over the dough. Gently knead five or six times until the dough has come together. Less is more. Pat the dough to one-half-inch thick. Cut with a biscuit cutter. Place biscuits on a baking sheet and bake about 12–15 minutes until they are light golden brown. Remove from oven and drizzle glaze over the tops. Serve warm.

Makes about 12 biscuits.

Quick Apple Shortcake

This was a favorite treat when I was a kid. In the fall when apples were plentiful, my mother would mix up a batch of biscuit dough, top it with sliced apples and drizzle with icing. It's quick, simple, frugal and wonderful.

This is a great recipe for kids to make. Younger children may need help with peeling and slicing the apples, but other than that, this recipe is almost foolproof for the beginner.

3/4 cup sugar
1/2 teaspoon cinnamon
1/4 cup (1/2 stick) butter
4 teaspoons baking powder
1/2 teaspoon salt
2 cups all-purpose flour
1 cup confectioner's sugar
3/4 cup milk plus 2–3 teaspoons
3–4 baking apples, peeled, cored and thinly (1/8") sliced

Preheat oven to 400°F.

Mix flour, salt, baking powder and one-half cup of sugar together in a large mixing bowl. Cut in butter using a pastry cutter. Stir in three-quarters of a cup of milk just until moistened. Press into 13x9 inch pan. Layer apple slices to cover the dough.

Mix cinnamon and remaining sugar and sprinkle over the top. Bake about 15–20 minutes until dough begins to brown. Mix together confectioner's sugar and drizzle over top.

Serve warm or cold.

Makes about 20 pieces.

Doughnuts

Homemade doughnuts were one of my favorite childhood treats. The doughnuts my father made would most accurately be described as fried cakes. They were batter doughnuts flavored with nutmeg, which we dusted with powdered or cinnamon sugar.

It seems as if you can't turn a corner without seeing a doughnut shop these days. Unfortunately, most of these establishments are more concerned about their coffee than their doughnuts. Their products don't come close to the wonderful flavor of a freshly made doughnut.

There are several basic varieties of doughnuts. They can be made with a batter, raised yeast dough, or a non-yeasted dough.

Frying doughnuts is definitely not kid stuff. They can help with making the dough, rolling, cutting and glazing. The baked version is a much better alternative for the young or novice doughnut maker.

❧ YEAST RAISED DOUGHNUTS ❧

This recipe produces doughnuts that are light, soft and tender. They are great glazed, but can be coated with confectioner's sugar or cinnamon sugar. To save time for freshly cooked doughnuts in the morning, the dough can be prepared the day before.

1 cup milk 1 egg, beaten
1/3 cup sugar 1 teaspoon salt
1 teaspoon vanilla 1 tablespoon yeast
2 tablespoons butter 1/4 teaspoon nutmeg
3 cups all-purpose flour

Glaze
1/4 cup milk
1/2 teaspoon vanilla
2 cups confectioner's sugar

Scald milk (see note on page 120). Pour scalded milk into mixing bowl. Stir in butter, sugar and salt. Cool to lukewarm.

Dissolve yeast in a quarter-cup of water. Add egg, vanilla and yeast. Beat in flour and nutmeg to form dough. Knead until soft and elastic. Grease a bowl. Put dough into bowl greasing the top as well. Cover and let rise until double in bulk.

Punch down dough. If you wish to finish the doughnuts the next day, cover dough with plastic wrap and refrigerate. Otherwise, turn dough out onto floured work surface. Gently roll the dough out one-quarter-inch thick. Cut with a doughnut cutter. Cover and let rise until double (the holes too). Mix the glaze.

Heat oil in a deep fryer or deep skillet to 350°F.

Fry doughnuts a few at a time until golden brown, turning to cook both sides. This should only take a couple of minutes. Use a thermometer to make sure temperature of oil recovers between batches. Drain on absorbent paper.

While still warm, dip doughnuts in glaze. Flip and place on rack to cool and allow glaze to flow over the doughnut.

If you prefer not to glaze they are great plain or dust with sugar or cinnamon sugar by shaking them in a bag with the sugar.

Variation

Baked Doughnuts: to save on the fat and calories, try baking the doughnuts. It's also easier.

Roll the dough a bit thicker, three-eights- to one-half-inch thick. After cutting out the doughnuts, place on greased baking sheets to rise. Preheat oven to 450°F. Place rack in top third of the oven.

When double in bulk, brush with egg wash made from one egg beaten with a dash of salt.

Bake 8–10 minutes until light golden brown.

Remove from pan and cool on rack until you can handle them. Dip in glaze. Flip and place on rack to allow glaze to flow over doughnut. These are best eaten warm.

Reheat leftover individual doughnuts in a microwave for 10–15 seconds. They will taste like they're right out of the oven.

Makes about 12 doughnuts.

Buttermilk Doughnuts

2 eggs	1/2 cup sugar
1 cup buttermilk	1/2 teaspoon salt
1 tablespoon vanilla	1/2 cup brown sugar
1/2 teaspoon nutmeg	4 cups all-purpose flour
1 teaspoon baking soda	1 teaspoon baking powder

1/4 cup (1/2 stick) melted butter

In a large mixing bowl, beat together the sugars and eggs. Beat in butter and buttermilk. In a separate bowl, mix together remaining dry ingredients. Add this to first mixture and beat together to make a stiff batter. Cover and refrigerate overnight.

Remove the dough and place on a well floured work surface. The dough will be sticky, but roll out one-quarter-inch thick. Cut with doughnut cutter. Deep fry at 375°F until golden brown, flipping doughnuts over to cook each side. Drain on absorbent paper. When cool, shake in a paper bag with cinnamon sugar of confectioner's sugar to coat, or eat them plain.

Makes about 12 doughnuts.

Beignets

This is my version of a New Orleans trademark. Eat them hot with a fresh cup of coffee or a big glass of ice-cold milk.

1 cup milk	1/4 cup sugar
2 eggs, beaten	1/2 cup butter
1/2 teaspoon salt	2 teaspoons vanilla
1 tablespoon yeast	1/2 teaspoons sugar
1/4 cup warm water	1/2 teaspoon nutmeg

3-1/2 cups all-purpose flour

Scald milk (see note on page 120). Place scalded milk in large bowl with sugar, butter and salt and let cool to lukewarm. Add yeast and one-half teaspoon of sugar to warm water. Whisk eggs and vanilla into milk. Stir in flour and nutmeg. Beat until dough starts to form. Turn out on to a floured surface and knead 5–7 minutes, adding more flour as needed until you get a soft, smooth and slightly sticky dough. Cover and let rise for an hour or refrigerate overnight. Roll out dough on a floured surface until one-eighth-inch thick. Cut into two-and-a-half-inch squares or triangles. Deep fry at 375°F until light golden brown, flipping over half way through cooking. Remove and drain on absorbent paper and dust with confectioner's sugar. Serve immediately.

Makes about 24 pieces.

Yeasted Breads

I love to make bread. I've tried countless recipes over the years. On occasion, I'll still pull out a more exotic one to make for a special occasion or just for fun. The few basic recipes below serve me for just about every normal use by simply varying the amount of sugar, the shape and additions and glazes. Master the sweet dough and Italian dough and you can make a lot of folks happy for a long time.

I use bread flour for most yeasted breads. It has more protein than all-purpose flour and therefore develops stronger gluten. I stopped measuring flour when making bread years ago. I use as much flour as is needed to achieve the proper consistency. The measurements in the recipes below are guidelines.

I buy bulk yeast, but if you use packets, use one packet per tablespoon of yeast called for in the recipe. Yeast loves a warm environment, so don't put warm water or milk into an ice-cold bowl; preheat the bowl first with hot water. Yeast needs food, so when I mix yeast with water, I add a half teaspoon of sugar. If you are using eggs, let them come up to room temperature. Yeast doesn't like too much salt, but salt is important in developing proteins in bread. Therefore, I add the salt after I've combined the yeast with other liquids and some flour. You can knead by hand or with an electric mixer, either way is fine. I also like to let the dough rest for a minute or two before I start to knead and again after about five minutes. This allows the gluten to relax and form properly.

Bread is easy! Relax and have fun!

Note on Scalding Milk

For the dough to behave properly, milk needs to be scalded to the proper temperature. Tests indicate that one minute at 198°F. or seven minutes at 185°F. will alter the milk proteins so that they will react properly with the flour proteins to produce a quality dough.

Failure to heat the milk sufficiently may cause the dough to be "slack".

Basic Sweet Bread Dough

This is my favorite standard bread dough. It's a sweet bread made with milk and sugar. Depending on what I'm using it for, I'll add more or less sugar.

I like the texture better without egg, but if you prefer a finer crumb and a golden color, use eggs.

Since these breads seem to disappear as fast as I can make them, I usually make a double batch.

1/2 cup sugar	1-1/4 cups milk
2 tablespoons yeast	1-1/2 teaspoons salt
4–5 cups bread flour	1 egg, beaten (optional)
1/4 cup lukewarm water	1/4 cup (1/2 stick) butter

Put milk into a saucepan and scald milk (see note above). Remove from heat, add butter and sugar and stir. Let cool to lukewarm.

In a large mixing bowl, put in the warm water, a half teaspoon of sugar and yeast. Whisk to dissolve yeast and place in warm place until yeast becomes foamy. When milk mixture is lukewarm, add to yeast. Add beaten egg (optional). Beat in a cup of flour until smooth. Add salt and beat in. Continue to add flour until a soft dough forms.

Turn dough out onto floured surface and knead 7–10 minutes until smooth and elastic, adding flour as necessary. Place in a large oiled bowl, cover and let rise in a warm place until double in bulk.

Punch down dough, then shape into loaves or rolls.

Swiss Braid

1 egg well beaten
1 batch sweet bread dough

Preheat oven to 425°F.

Punch down the risen dough and divide in half. Divide each half into thirds. Roll each piece into a rope about 18 inches long. Make two braids using three ropes per braid. Put first braid on a greased baking sheet. Brush top of braid with egg. Place second braid on top of first.

Brush entire loaf with egg. Cover loosely with plastic wrap and let rise until double. Remove wrap, sprinkle with sugar if desired and place into preheated oven. Reduce oven to 375°F and bake for 20–25 minutes.

When done, remove from oven and transfer to wire rack to cool.

Makes 1 loaf.

Dinner Rolls

1 egg well beaten (optional)
sesame or poppy seeds (optional)
1 batch of sweet roll dough* (see recipe on page 139)

Preheat oven to 425°F.

Punch down risen dough. Spray a 13x9-inch pan with non-stick cooking spray. With your thumb and forefinger, pull up a corner of the dough. With a small, sharp knife, cut off a small piece and form into a ball about the size of a golf ball. Put seam side down in the pan. You should get about 2 dozen rolls.

If desired, brush rolls with egg and if desired, sprinkle with seeds or sugar. Cover loosely with plastic wrap and let rise until double.

Remove wrap and place in oven. Bake 12–15 minutes until done. Remove from pan and let cool on wire rack.

Makes 2 dozen rolls.

*I usually use a bit less sugar for the dinner roll dough, one-quarter instead of one-half cup.

Orange Rolls

An historic restaurant, just up the road, serves rolls very much like this. They've been around since 1808. Hopefully some of their charm will rub off on us!

1 orange
1/2 cup sugar
1 recipe sweet bread dough
6 tablespoon melted butter

Preheat oven to 425°F.

Carefully peel the zest off the surface of the orange avoiding the removal of the white part of the skin. With a sharp knife, mince this very finely. Then squeeze the juice out of the orange and reserve for the glaze. On a floured surface, roll out the dough into a rectangle 24 inches long by 12 inches wide. Brush with melted butter, sprinkle with sugar and scatter the orange peel over the entire area. Roll the dough up to get a 24-inch-long log. Pinch the seam to seal the edge. Spray two muffin pans with non-stick cooking spray. Cut into 24 slices and put each one into a muffin cup. Bake 12–15 minutes until done. Remove from oven and transfer the rolls to a wire rack. Let cool slightly and then drizzle with the orange glaze.

Orange Glaze
1/4 cup orange juice
2 cups confectioner's sugar

Stir together until glaze is smooth. Drizzle over warm rolls.

Makes 2 dozen rolls.

Cinnamon Raisin Bread

You have several options with this. You can bake this in regular loaf pans or a round casserole. I often braid it. Icing is optional, but desirable.

1 cup raisins
1 tablespoon cinnamon
1 recipe sweet bread dough

Preheat oven to 425°F.

Punch down risen dough. Flatten slightly and sprinkle with cinnamon and raisins. Fold over dough to envelop raisins and knead lightly to incorporate the raisins. Put back in greased bowl and let dough relax for about 10 minutes. Remove from bowl and shape as desired. Cover with plastic wrap and let rise until double.

Remove plastic wrap. Put the loaf into your preheated oven and reduce heat to 375°F. (Starting the loaf at the higher temperature generates more "oven spring" for a lighter loaf. Reducing the temperature for the remainder of the baking prevents over-browning.) Bake about 25–30 minutes until the loaf reaches an internal temperature of 200°F. Remove from baking sheet and cool on wire rack. If desired, ice cooled loaf with a mixture of one cup of confectioner's sugar, two tablespoons of milk and a half-teaspoon of vanilla.

Makes 1 loaf.

Italian Bread Dough

This is a simple dough. But there is often beauty in simplicity. I usually make a double batch. It freezes well so when you want to make a pizza (see recipe on page 170) all you have to do is pull out the dough and thaw.

2 teaspoons salt
1 tablespoon yeast
1-1/2 cups lukewarm water
1 teaspoon sugar
3-1/2–4 cups of flour
1-2 tablespoon olive oil to taste

In a large mixing bowl, put in water, sugar and yeast. Whisk to dissolve yeast and place in warm spot. When foamy, whisk in one cup of flour and olive oil and mix until smooth. Add salt and another cup of flour and mix. Continue to stir in flour until a soft dough forms. Turn onto floured surface and knead 7–10 minutes until dough becomes smooth and elastic adding additional flour as needed. If freezing, put into oiled Ziploc bag, removing as much excess air as possible. If using right away, put in oiled bowl, cover and let rise in a warm place until doubled in bulk. This recipe can also be used to make focaccia.

Garlic Bread Sticks

1/4 teaspoon salt
1 teaspoon garlic powder
1/4 cup melted butter
1 recipe Italian bread dough

Preheat oven to 425F.

Punch down risen dough and divide into 12 equal pieces. Roll each piece into a rope about three-eighth inch in diameter. Place sideways on a baking sheet allowing space for each stick to rise without touching. Cover with plastic wrap and let rise until double. Remove plastic and bake 8–10 minutes or until done. Remove from oven. Add garlic powder and salt to melted butter. Brush on breadsticks and serve immediately.

Makes 12 pieces.

Italian Bread

1 recipe Italian bread dough (recipe on preceding page)

Preheat oven to 425°F.

If you have a pizza stone use it. Punch down risen dough. Shape into oblong or round loaf. Slash top with a sharp knife or razor blade; for a loaf one cut down the length of the loaf, if round, three slashes about an inch apart. Cover and let rise until doubled.

The key to a crusty loaf is moisture in the oven. A half cup of water and a few ice cubes will do the trick. I have an electric oven, so I can just toss the ice water onto the bottom of the oven. If you have gas, a heavy pan on the bottom rack will work.

Slide the loaf off the peel onto the stone, or leave on baking sheet and put onto stone. Toss in ice water combo and quickly close the oven door. Depending on the shape of the loaf, bake 20–30 minutes until done. Remove from oven and cool on wire rack.

Makes 1 loaf.

Country Fair Egg Bread

My father always made this bread for the traditional Christmas Eve ham sandwiches. Eggy, with a very fine, dense crumb, this bread makes great toast. This will make two large loaves. It can also be shaped into rolls.

2 cups milk
2 tablespoon yeast
9–10 cups bread flour
4 eggs beaten
1 cup lukewarm water
1/2 cup (1 stick) butter
2 tablespoon plus 2 teaspoons sugar

Preheat oven to 425°F.

Put milk into a saucepan and scald milk (see note on page 139). Remove from heat, add butter and sugar and stir. Let cool to lukewarm. In a large mixing bowl, put in the warm water, a half teaspoon of sugar and yeast. Whisk to dissolve yeast and place in warm place until yeast becomes foamy. When milk mixture is lukewarm, add to yeast. Add beaten eggs. Beat in a couple of cups of flour until smooth. Add salt and beat in. Continue to add flour until a soft dough forms. Turn out onto floured surface and knead 7–10 minutes until smooth and elastic, adding flour as necessary. Place in a large bowl, cover and let rise until doubled. Punch down then shape into loaves or rolls. Cover and let rise until doubled. Put into in preheated oven. For bread, reduce heat to 375°F and bake 30–40 minutes until done. For rolls, keep oven at 425°F and bake 12–15 minutes until done. Remove from pans and cool on a wire rack.

Makes 2 loaves or 48 rolls.

Cheddar Twist Bread

This is a fun bread to make when you want something that is both eye-catching and full of flavor. It is a wonderfully soft bread marbled with the smooth richness of the cheddar. I recommend a sharp cheddar. If you are concerned about your salt intake, you can skip the coarse salt on the outside, but it really adds to the character of the loaf.

3 eggs
1/3 cup sugar
coarse sea salt
2 teaspoons salt
4–5 cups bread flour
1-1/2 cups warm water
1 tablespoons dry yeast
2 tablespoons melted butter
2 tablespoons grated parmesan
3 cups shredded sharp cheddar cheese

Put warm water into a large mixing bowl. Add a teaspoon of sugar and yeast. Stir to dissolve the yeast and place bowl in a warm spot until yeast begins to foam. When yeast is foamy, beat in a heaping cup of flour and mix until smooth. Add salt, eggs melted butter and one cup of the cheese and beat into the batter. Continue adding flour until a dough forms which is stiff enough to knead. Turn onto a floured surface and kneads for several minutes, adding flour as necessary until dough is smooth and elastic. Put dough into a greased bowl, cover and let rise in a warm place until doubled in bulk

Punch down dough and turn onto floured surface. Pat dough flat into a rough circle about 12 inches in diameter. Sprinkle one-and-a-half cups of cheese (reserving a half-cup for the topping) over the dough. Pull dough up and over the cheese and knead slightly to incorporate the cheese into the dough. Put back into greased bowl, cover and let rest about 15 minutes.

Turn dough back out onto floured surface and divide into three equal portions. Roll each piece into a rope about 18 inches long. Braid the dough and put onto a greased baking sheet. Cover and let rise in a warm place until doubled in bulk.

Preheat your oven to 425°F.

Once the loaf has risen, beat the remaining egg in a small dish. Brush the egg wash over the loaf with a pastry brush. Combine the remaining one-half cup of cheddar with the parmesan cheese and sprinkle over the loaf. Then sprinkle generously with the coarse sea salt.

Put the loaf into your preheated oven and reduce heat to 375°F. (Starting the loaf at the higher temperature generates more "oven spring" for a lighter loaf. Reducing the temperature for the remainder of the baking prevents over-browning.) Bake about 25–30 minutes until the loaf reaches an internal temperature of 200°F.

Remove from baking sheet and cool on wire rack.

Makes 1 loaf.

The Allens Hill Farm Cookbook

Quick Breads

Quick breads are perfect for supper. They can be prepared and baked in less than an hour. They do not use yeast for leavening, so no kneading or rising is required. Just stir a few ingredients together and bake.

Quick breads are ideal recipes for the young baker. They are almost foolproof. The techniques simply require accurate measuring, a quick stir and into the oven it goes.

Irish Soda Bread

This bread has an amazing aroma and wonderful golden crust. You can use fresh buttermilk instead of the dried powder and water. However, the dried buttermilk is very convenient since you can keep it on hand for whenever you need it.

2 eggs
1-1/2 cup raisins
3 cups all-purpose flour
1 tablespoon caraway seeds
1/4 cup sugar
1-1/2 teaspoons salt
1 teaspoon baking soda
1/2 cup buttermilk powder
1 tablespoon baking powder
1/2 cup (1 stick) butter at room temperature

Preheat oven to 350°F.

Liberally smear a 10-inch cast iron frying pan with two tablespoons of the butter. In a small saucepan, melt two tablespoons of the butter. In a small bowl beat the eggs and whisk in the water and melted butter. In another mixing bowl stir together all the remaining dry ingredients. Add the liquid to the dry and stir just enough to combine. Don't over-mix. Pour the batter into the prepared pan. Use the remaining four tablespoons of butter to dot the top with several pats of butter. Bake about 1 hour or until a toothpick inserted in the center comes out clean.

Makes 1 loaf.

ALLENS HILL FARM
APPLE CIDER MOLASSES CORNBREAD

This cornbread has a lovely amber color and the distinctive flavor of our signature Apple Cider Molasses.

1 cup milk
1 egg, beaten
1/2 teaspoon salt
1 cup all-purpose flour
1/4 cup oil
1/4 cup sugar
3/4 cup cornmeal
1 teaspoon baking soda
2 teaspoons baking powder
1/4 cup Allens Hill Farm Apple Cider Molasses

Preheat the oven to 425°F.

Mix dry ingredients together in a mixing bowl. Add remaining ingredients and blend well. Pour batter into a 8x8-inch pan. Bake for 20–25 minutes or until a toothpick inserted in center comes out clean. For best apple flavor, when cool, cover and allow to mellow overnight before serving.

Makes 9 pieces.

CORN BREAD

This is a more traditional corn bread recipe. Yankees like me prefer our cornbread on the sweeter side, but if ya'll want it like mama used to make, just omit the sugar. The recipe makes a 13x9-inch pan. If you want to use an 8 x 8-inch pan, cut the recipe in half.

2 eggs
2 cups milk
1 teaspoon salt
1-1/2 cup yellow cornmeal
1/2 cup oil
1 cup sugar
2 cups all-purpose flour
3 tablespoons baking powder

Preheat the oven to 425°F.

Grease your pan with non-stick cooking spray. Mix dry ingredients in a mixing bowl. Add eggs, oil and milk. Mix well. Pour batter into 13x9 inch pan. Bake 25 minutes or until a toothpick inserted in the center comes out clean. The corn bread will become more moist if you bake this the night before and cover when cool.

Makes about 20 pieces.

EASY NON-FAT WHOLE WHEAT BREAD

This is the easiest whole wheat bread recipe you'll ever find. It also makes a great after school snack. Allens Hill Farm Apple Cider Molasses is the secret to producing moist bread without oil or eggs.

1 teaspoon salt	1-1/2 cups water
1/2 cup cornmeal	1 teaspoon baking soda
1/3 cup buttermilk powder	2-1/4 cups whole wheat flour
1/2 cup Allens Hill Farm Apple Cider Molasses	

Preheat oven to 325°F. Lightly grease a loaf pan. Put dry ingredients into a mixing bowl. Stir to combine. Add liquid ingredients and mix until just combined. Pour into loaf pan and bake about 1 hour until a toothpick inserted in the center comes out clean. Cool on rack. If you bake this a day ahead and wrap when cool, it will become wonderfully moist by the next day. This bread will stay fresh for days.

Makes 1 loaf.

Garlic Cheese Biscuits

Some years ago, I managed a well-known restaurant, with garlic cheese biscuits as their signature item. The original biscuits make use of hard-to-duplicate commercial baking ingredients. This recipe is a fairly good facsimile using ingredients for the home baker. They must be pretty close since my crew clamors for me to make them all of the time. This recipe yields about 20 biscuits.

1 cup water	1/2 teaspoon salt
1/2 cup shortening	1 tablespoon sugar
1/2 teaspoon baking soda	1/4 cup buttermilk powder
4 teaspoons baking powder	2-1/4 cups all-purpose flour
2 cups shredded cheddar cheese	

Preheat oven to 425°F. In a mixing bowl combine all the dry ingredients except the cheese. Stir to combine. Add the shortening and cut in using a pastry cutter or your fingers. The texture should resemble peas. Add the cheese and water and stir until just combined. This dough is very sticky. The best way to portion is with a one-and-a-half-ounce ice cream scoop. If you don't have one, then spoon out onto a baking sheet sprayed with non-stick cooking spray in lumps about the size of a lime. Bake about 15 minutes until done and they are a nice golden brown.

While they are baking, prepare the garlic butter topping.

Garlic Butter Topping

| 1/2 stick butter | 1/2 teaspoon salt |
| 1 teaspoon parsley flakes | 1-1/2 teaspoons garlic powder |

Melt butter and add garlic powder, parsley flakes and salt. Stir to combine.

As soon as you remove the biscuits from the oven, brush the tops liberally with the garlic butter topping. Serve immediately.

Makes about 24 biscuits.

The Allens Hill Farm Cookbook

Desserts

Aunt Mildred's Camp Cookies
Recipe on page 153.

 ## Cakes

QUICK AND MOIST CHOLESTEROL-FREE CHOCOLATE CAKE

This cake requires neither butter nor eggs and has no cholesterol when made with water instead of milk. Make as a layer cake, a sheet or bundt. You an also cut this recipe in half for an 8x8 inch pan or for a single layer cake.

>   2 cups sugar   1 teaspoon salt
>   2 teaspoons vanilla   2 tablespoons vinegar
>   2/3 cup vegetable oil 1/2 cup cocoa powder
>   3 cups all-purpose flour 2 teaspoons baking soda
>   2 cups cold water or milk, or —if you're going for the Dr. Pepper frosting, —use
>   1 cup Dr. Pepper and 1 cup milk

Preheat oven to 350°F. Mix all dry ingredients in a bowl. Add oil, liquid, vanilla and vinegar last. Stir well and pour into prepared pan(s) of your choice. Bake until done; bundt about 50 minutes; 13x9-inch pan or layer pan 25–35 minutes. Remove and place on wire rack to cool. Either dust with confectioners sugar or frost.

Makes about 20 pieces.

This recipe is inspired by the Dinosaur BBQ cookbook. (one of my favorites). The frosting cancels out the "no cholesterol" advantage, but it sure is good.

Dr. Pepper Frosting

>   Dash of salt   1/4 cup Dr. Pepper
>   6 tablespoons butter   1/4 cup cocoa powder
>   4 cups confectioner's sugar 2 teaspoon vanilla extract
>   3/4 cup vegetable shortening

Beat butter, shortening and salt until fluffy. Add cocoa and sugar and combine with butter. Add vanilla and slowly pour in Dr. Pepper while beating on high speed until light and fluffy.

Peanut Butter Frosting

>   1/3 cup milk   1/2 cup (1 stick) butter
>   4 cups confectioner's sugar 2 teaspoons vanilla extract
>   1 cup smooth peanut butter

Beat together butter and peanut butter until light and fluffy. Slowly beat in two cups of the sugar, and then add most of the milk. Continue beating and add remaining sugar. Add more milk if needed to achieve desired consistency.

🌾 Pound Cake 🌿

This is a family favorite. The recipe is adapted from Julia Child's "Baking with Julia."

1 cup milk	2 cups sugar
1/2 teaspoon salt	3 large eggs, beaten
1 cup (2 sticks) butter	3 cups all-purpose flour
2 teaspoons vanilla extract	2 teaspoons baking powder

Preheat oven to 350°F.

Put oven rack in the lower third of the oven. Butter and flour either a 10-inch tube pan or bundt pan. Allow butter and milk to come to room temperature. In a bowl combine flour, salt and baking powder; set aside.

Beat butter with an electric mixer at medium speed until smooth. Keep beating and pour in the sugar in a steady stream. Beat at medium speed 4–5 minutes, occasionally scraping down side of bowl, until light and fluffy. Continue beating and slowly add the eggs over a period of 4 minutes until mixture is light colored, fluffy and not shiny.

Reduce speed to low and stir in flour mixture and milk, alternating the two, four additions of flour and three of milk. The batter should be smooth before the next addition. Scrape the bowl frequently to insure all ingredients are incorporated. After last addition, mix until smooth. Add vanilla and stir to incorporate.

Put batter into pan and smooth the top. Bake 50–60 minutes or until a toothpick inserted in the center comes out clean. Let cool on wire rack for about 10 minutes, then invert pan to remove the cake. Let cool before slicing.

Great with fresh berries and whipped cream or ice cream and chocolate sauce.

Makes about 24 pieces.

🌾 Spice Cake 🌿

This is a very traditional American cake: lots of wonderful, warm spices in a dense moist cake. This version is made a bit more authentic with the addition of Allens Hill Farm Apple Cider Molasses and raisins. The Allens Hill Farm Spice Cake Mix is even more interesting in that we use a combination of flours including oat flour and buckwheat flour.

Make this cake a day ahead. The spices flavor through the cake as it sits. It's also great with a butter cream frosting.

Note: if you wish to substitute fresh buttermilk in place of water, just omit the buttermilk powder.

2 eggs	1 teaspoon salt
1-1/4 cup water	1-1/2 cups sugar
1 teaspoon vanilla	1 teaspoon nutmeg
1/2 teaspoon cloves	1/2 cup vegetable oil
1/2 teaspoon allspice	3 cups all-purpose flour
1/2 cup raisins (optional)	1/3 cup buttermilk powder
1-1/2 teaspoons cinnamon	1-1/2 teaspoons baking soda

1/2 cup Allens Hill Farm Apple Cider Molasses

Preheat oven to 350°F.

Grease and flour your pan(s). You can use either a 13x9-inch pan, two 9-inch round pans or a bundt pan.

In a mixing bowl, add all the dry ingredients and stir to combine. Add all of the wet ingredients and beat for about one minute to combine. Stir in raisins. Pour batter into pan and bake in oven.

Bake layers and 13x9 cake for 30–40 minutes; bake a bundt cake 50–60 minutes or until a toothpick inserted in the center comes out clean. Remove and let cool on wire rack about ten minutes. Remove from pan and let cool completely before frosting.

Makes about 20 pieces.

Allens Hill Farm
Apple Cider Molasses Gingerbread

The Apple Cider Molasses really gives this gingerbread a wonderful flavor, color and texture. Be sure to bake a day ahead since the flavor and moistness really develop as it rests. Be sure to serve with lots of fresh whipped cream.

2 eggs	3/4 cup sugar
1/2 teaspoon salt	3/4 cup boiling water
2 cups all-purpose flour	2 teaspoons ginger powder
1-1/2 teaspoons baking soda	1 stick (1/2 cup) softened butter

1/2 cup Allens Hill Farm Apple Cider Molasses

Preheat oven to 350°F.

Butter and flour a 9-inch round cake pan. Beat butter and sugar together. Add Allens Hill Farm Apple Cider Molasses and boiling water. Stir to melt butter. Sift together remaining dry ingredients. When liquid mixture reaches room temperature, add dry ingredients and eggs. Mix thoroughly. Pour into pan. Bake 40–45 minutes until toothpick inserted in center comes out clean. Cool on rack.

Makes about 10 pieces.

Cookies

If you have kids you have to get them involved in cookie making. This is a time to have fun and get them excited about being in the kitchen. Teach them how to properly measure. When they are of age, it's a great time to teach oven safety and baking basics. Besides, what kid doesn't like to lick the bowl?

⌇ Big Chewy Chocolate Chip Cookies ⌇

Some people like their chocolate chip cookies small and crisp. No way! Not for me! These are big. The addition of a bit of corn syrup really lends chewiness. They are loaded with chips. When my son makes these cookies he likes to break up a Hershey's Symphony bar and add it for the toffee flavor and crunch. Feel free to use chips or chunks, milk, semi-sweet or bittersweet or a combination.

2 eggs
1/2 teaspoon salt
1 pound chocolate chips
1 tablespoon vanilla extract
3/4 cup sugar
3 cups all-purpose flour
3/4 cup light brown sugar
1 tablespoon baking powder
3 tablespoons light corn syrup
1 cup (2 sticks) butter at room temperature

In a bowl combine flour, baking powder and salt and set aside. Get out your electric mixer and beat together the butter, sugar, brown sugar and corn syrup. When, after a couple of minutes, this is light and fluffy, add the eggs and vanilla and beat until combined. Add half the flour mixture and stir until combined. Add the remaining flour and a heaping cup of the chocolate. Mix until well combined. Chill the dough for about a half an hour until it is firm enough to handle.

Preheat oven to 375°F.

Form dough into balls about the size of a golf ball. I use a one-and-a-half-ounce ice cream scoop. Take the remaining chocolate and place in a shallow dish or plate. Press each ball into the chocolate chips or chunks then place onto greased cookie sheets, chip side up. Press down until slightly flattened.

Bake 10–12 minutes, rotating pans after about six minutes to insure even cooking. Remove when slightly brown at the edges; don't over-bake. Transfer to wire rack to cool.

Makes 2 dozen.

Aunt Mildred's Camp Cookies

When Aunt Mildred would call my mom and ask us to come up to her camp to go swimming, I was more excited about these cookies than the lake. Imagine a soft, chewy gingersnap that you want to eat by the dozen…that's why this is a big batch. Feel free to cut this recipe in half. I added my own twist by using Allens Hill Farm Apple Cider Molasses instead of regular light molasses.

2 eggs
1-1/2 cups butter
4 cups all-purpose flour
1 teaspoon ginger powder
1 teaspoon salt
2 teaspoons cinnamon
4 teaspoons baking soda
2 cups sugar plus extra for rolling
1/2 cup Allens Hill Farm Apple Cider Molasses

Preheat the oven to 375°F.

In a bowl combine flour, salt, spices and soda. Set aside. Using an electric mixer beat together butter and sugar. When well-combined, add molasses and beat well. Add egg and beat to combine. Stir in flour mixture and mix until well-combined.

Roll dough into balls the size of a large marble. Put some sugar in a shallow bowl or plate and roll balls until coated.

Place balls on greased cookie sheets. Bake 8-10 minutes rotating the trays after 5 minutes. Cookies will be cracked on top and slightly puffy; don't over-bake (or you'll get gingersnaps). Transfer to wire rack and let cool.

Makes 6 dozen.

Grandma's Molasses Cookies

My grandmother always had a tin in her kitchen cupboard with these cookies inside. They are old-fashioned goodness personified. Even better after they have mellowed for a day, grab a big glass of ice cold milk and enjoy these big, soft beauties.

1 egg
1/2 teaspoon salt
sugar for sprinkling
1/2 teaspoon ginger
1/8 teaspoon allspice
1 stick (1/2 cup butter)
1/2 teaspoon cinnamon
1/2 cup water
raisins for garnish
1/4 teaspoon cloves
1/2 cup brown sugar
1/4 teaspoon nutmeg
3 cups all-purpose flour
1-1/2 teaspoons baking soda
3/4 cup Allens HIll Farm Apple Cider Molasses

Place salt, brown sugar, butter and molasses in a saucepan. Bring to a boil. Add water and let cool to room temperature. Add egg and mix thoroughly. Combine remaining dry ingredients. Add to cooled liquid mixture. Chill dough until firm (a few hours or overnight).

Preheat oven to 375°F.

Grease cookie sheets. Scoop dough into balls the size of golf balls. Pat with floured hands into discs about three-eighths-inch thick. Place onto cookie sheets maximum six per sheet; these get very big. Sprinkle with sugar and garnish with raisins if desired.

Bake 8–10 minutes until center of cookie is firm. Cool on racks.

Makes about 18 cookies.

Mom's Peanut Butter Cookies

These were my favorite cookies as a kid. Feel free to play around with these. I like crunchy peanut butter versus smooth. Feel free to add some roasted peanuts, chocolate or other flavored chips. Adding the optional corn syrup makes the cookies chewier.

2 eggs
1 teaspoon vanilla
1 cup brown sugar
1 cup butter (2 sticks)
1 cup sugar
1/2 teaspoon salt
1 cup peanut butter
3 cups all-purpose flour
1-1/2 teaspoons baking soda
2 tablespoons light corn syrup (optional)

Preheat oven to 375°F.

In a bowl combine flour, soda and salt. Beat butter, sugar and brown sugar with an electric mixer until fluffy. Beat in eggs and vanilla. Stir in flour mixture until well combined. Stir in peanut butter (hint spray your measuring cup with non-stick cooking spray before measuring peanut butter). You may have to finish mixing in peanut butter by hand.

Roll dough into balls about one inch in diameter. Place balls onto ungreased cookie sheets. Flatten balls with a fork dipped in flour by pressing down once and then again with the fork at 90° to form a criss-cross pattern.

Bake 8–10 minutes. Transfer to wire rack and cool.

Makes about 48 cookies.

Katherine's Date Cookies

This recipe has been handed down from my grandmother. These date cookies are moist. Since they are baked in a pan and then cut, they are also easy to make.

2 eggs
1-1/2 cup sugar
1/2 cup hot water
1 teaspoon baking soda
1/2 cup shredded coconut
1/2 cup vegetable shortening
1 cup chopped walnuts or pecans
1 teaspoon salt
1 teaspoon vanilla
2-1/4 cups bread flour
1 pound of chopped dates
1 teaspoon baking powder
confectioner's sugar for dusting

Preheat oven to 350°F. In a bowl mix together flour, salt and baking powder; set aside. Mix baking soda into hot water and let cool to lukewarm. Beat together shortening and sugar with electric mixer. Add eggs and vanilla; beat to combine. Add water and stir. Stir in flour mixture and mix until well combined. Stir in dates, coconut and nuts. Spray a 13x9-inch pan with non-stick cooking spray. Spoon in the batter and smooth the top. Bake 35–40 minutes or until a toothpick inserted in the center comes out clean. Let cool. Dust with confectioner's sugar and cut into one-inch square cookies.

Makes about 8 dozen cookies.

Wheat-Free Oatmeal Cookies

These oatmeal cookies have a great oat flavor when they are made with oat flour instead of wheat flour, but if you don't have oat flour, wheat flour is fine, although then they won't be wheat-free. I also like lots of raisins, but if you don't, leave them out, or substitute chocolate chips or dried cranberries. Use thick rolled oats, not instant or quick oats.

1 egg
1 cup oat flour
1/4 teaspoon salt
1/2 cup brown sugar
1/2 teaspoon cinnamon
1-1/2 cups thick rolled oats
1/2 cup sugar
1/2 cup raisins
1 teaspoons vanilla
1/2 cup (1 stick butter)
1/4 teaspoon baking soda
1/4 teaspoon baking powder

Preheat oven to 375°F.

In a bowl combine oats, oat flour, cinnamon, salt, baking powder and soda. Beat butter, sugar and brown sugar with an electric mixer until light and fluffy. Beat in egg and vanilla. (If you like your cookies on the thin side, add a tablespoon of water.). Stir in flour mixture until well-combined. Stir in raisins.

Drop by tablespoons full onto greased cookie sheet. Bake 9–11 minutes or until done. Transfer to wire rack to cool.

Makes about 18 cookies.

Soft Sugar Cookies

These big cookies are incredibly light and fluffy thanks to the buttermilk. Remember, you can substitute the cup of buttermilk with a quarter-cup of buttermilk powder and one cup of water.

2 eggs
1-1/2 cup sugar
1 teaspoon nutmeg
3 cups all-purpose flour
1 tablespoon vanilla extract
1 teaspoon salt
1 cup buttermilk
1 teaspoon baking soda
1 cup vegetable shortening
1 tablespoon baking powder

Preheat oven to 450°F. Combine flour, salt baking powder and soda and nutmeg in a bowl and set aside. Beat together shortening and sugar with an electric mixer until fluffy. Beat in eggs and vanilla. Add half the flour, stir to combine. Then add buttermilk, stir and then add remaining flour. Mix until well-combined. Spoon generous tablespoons of dough onto greased cookie sheets and sprinkle tops with sugar. Bake 8–10 minutes or until cookies begin to brown on the edges. Transfer to wire racks to cool.

Makes about 2 dozen cookies.

Grandma's Molasses Cookies
Recipe on page 153.

Other Desserts

➤ 8 GRAIN BLACK FOREST BROWNIE SUNDAE ➤

1 cup water
vanilla ice cream
dash of cinnamon
1/2 cup sugar or to taste
whippped cream (optional)
1/4 cup brandy or kirsch (optional)
Allens Hill Farm 8 Grain Brownie Mix
1 quart fresh tart cherries, pitted and split

Bake brownies according to directions. While brownies are baking, put water and cherries in a saucepan and cook over medium high heat until tender, about 20 minutes. Reduce heat and add remaining ingredients. Remove from heat. Cut brownies and place onto plates. Top with a scoop of ice cream and spoon cherries over the top. Garnish with whipped cream.

Makes about 16 servings.

➤ APPLE OATMEAL CRUMBLE ➤

This is a great dessert and also an excellent side dish with a roast ham or pork. I also like to add some raisins when I'm in the mood. The apples are important too. A tart, firm apple is a good choice, like a Twenty-Ounce or Cortland. If you want to make this fat-free, simply omit the butter in the filling and use some apple cider in place of butter in the topping.

Preheat oven to 325°F. Spray a casserole dish with non-stick cooking spray.

Filling
1/2 cup sugar
2 tablespoons flour
1/4 teaspoon nutmeg
1/2 teaspoon cinnamon
2 tablespoons melted butter
6 cups apples (4–6) peeled and cut into 1/4–1/2 inch chunks

Toss ingredients together and put into casserole dish.

Topping

1/4 teaspoon salt	1/2 cups thick oats
1 teaspoon nutmeg	1 teaspoon cinnamon
1/2 cup all-purpose flour	1/2 cup light brown sugar

1/4 cup (1/2 stick) butter

Mix dry ingredients together in a small mixing bowl. Cut in butter as you would in making pie crust until combined. Spread over apples. Place into oven and bake 40–50 minutes until filling starts to bubble up. Serve warm with ice cream and whipped cream.

Makes 8 to 10 servings.

Cinnamon Baked Apples

sugar
4 large apples
Allens Hill Farm Apple Cinnamon Syrup

Preheat oven to 375°F. Peel and core the apples (Cortland or Ida Red). Place in baking pan with about one-half inch of water in bottom. Sprinkle with sugar (about one-quarter cup). Bake until tender; about 1 hour. Cool to room temperature. Drizzle with Allens Hill Farm Apple Cinnamon Syrup and serve with ice cream and or whipped cream.

Makes 4 servings.

Brownie Pecan Pie

Use Allens Hill Farm 8 Grain Brownie Mix to make a luscious brownie pecan pie that just screams to be topped with ice cream, chocolate sauce and whipped cream.

2 eggs	1/2 cup oil
1/4 cup water	1/2 cup pecans

1 package Allens Hill Farm 8 Grain Brownie Mix

Preheat over to 350°F. If you want the nuts to be a bit crunchier and more flavorful, toast for a few minutes in the oven and let cool. Prepare brownie mix as directed on the package, adding the nuts with the dry mix. (Or you can just press them into the top after you put them into the pan). Press mix into a greased 9-inch pie pan. Bake about 40 minutes until done. Let cool.

Cut into wedges and serve topped with ice cream, chocolate sauce and whipped cream.

Makes 10 servings.

Let's Party!

Appetizers, Munchies and Fun Food

Dukkah

Dukkah, a Middle Eastern food, is believed to have originated in Egypt. Pita bread was dipped in oil and then in the blend of nuts and spices.

Dukkah has become extremely popular in the culinary melting pot of New Zealand and Australia where its surge in popularity has been coupled with their exploding wine industry. It is only just becoming known in the United States.

The traditional way to enjoy dukkah is with a group of friends or family (see **Is it ok to dukkah alone?** below). You will need a bag of dukkah (of course), a good quality oil (olive is preferred), good bread (crusty loaves like Italian or a baguette, or the traditional pita), and a couple of dishes for the oil and dukkah. Simply dip the bread in the oil and then into the dukkah and enjoy.

Dukkah is absolutely the perfect compliment to a great bottle of wine or microbrew.

Dukkah Varieties

Allens Hill Farm's all natural varieties of dukkah are unique interpretations of traditional Egyptian nut and spice mixtures. We freshly roast pistachios and hazelnuts nuts then blend them together with freshly toasted sesame seeds and organic spices. There are no additives or preservatives used.

Down under Dukkah

Why do we call it Down under Dukkah? Well a good friend from Australia told us about this incredible food, which is a craze in her country. Down under Dukkah is a traditional savory blend of hazelnuts, pistachios, sesame seeds, cumin and coriander. The ultimate dipping dukkah also makes a great topping for meats, seafood and poultry. Sprinkle over salads to add flavor and crunch.

Dukkah Hazard

Caution: Dukkah at your own risk! Dukkah Hazard is not a dukkah for the faint of heart, but for those with true culinary courage. We turbo charge our traditional dukkah with garlic, smoked sea salt and cayenne pepper. Great with a robust wine, over fresh sliced tomatoes or add interest by sprinkling over pasta.

What You Always Wanted to Know About Dukkah But Were Afraid to Ask!

Can you dukkah in bed?

This would be considered an advanced technique, unsuited for beginners. Keeping the crumbs off the sheets calls for real dipping skill and the oil can be a distraction.

Can you dukkah alone?

Well, of course, you can, but the question is should you. It is certainly more fun to dukkah with others.

Can you dukkah outdoors?

Absolutely! In fact, we encourage it. There is no better place to dukkah than on your deck, patio or in the backyard.

Is there a minimum age to dukkah?

Actually, we'd love it if you can get your kids hooked at an early age. It is great way to promote family get gatherings, conversation and to broaden their culinary experience.

Is it legal to dukkah and drive?

Yes, but only because the government hasn't heard about it yet. Actually, it is not wise to dukkah and drive; there is nowhere to put the dishes.

What's the best time to dukkah?

Anytime is the right time. (How clichéd!) Dukkah is a great food to have on hand. It is flavorful, exotic and unique. It can be an instant appetizer or a marvelous way to perk up a tired old recipe.

Dukkah is absolutely outstanding with wine or your favorite beer.

Can you dukkah is the morning?

Traditionally dukkah is not a morning thing. Yet, Allens Hill Farm's, Let's Dukkah Breakfast, is a perfect way to turn your boring toast or bagel into a flavorful treat. It is also great sprinkled over yogurt or hot cereal.

Allens Hill Farm Dukkah

Party Food Recipes

❦ Sweet and Spicy Wings ❦

salt and pepper
bamboo skewers
1 dozen whole chicken wings
Allens Hill Farm Spiced Apple Glaze

Rinse wings and pat dry. Skewer three to four wings per skewer. Sprinkle with salt and pepper.

Grill or bake wings (in a 450°F oven) until they reach a minimum internal temperature of 165°F and skin is crisp. Brush wings liberally with Spiced Apple Glaze and cook a few more minutes until glaze is hot.

Makes 3 to 4 servings.

❦ Dukkah Wings ❦

honey
salt and pepper
bamboo skewers
Allens Hill Farm Dukkah Hazard
whole chicken wings (at least 3 per person)

Crank up your grill. Skewer the wings, three per skewer. Sprinkle liberally with salt and pepper.

Grill wings until well done (minimum internal temp 165°F) and skin is crisp. Remove from grill and brush lightly with honey. Sprinkle with Dukkah Hazard. Enjoy with an ice cold beverage.

Buffalo Wings

Having lived in and near Buffalo most of my life, I'm here to tell you that what most restaurants call Buffalo wings are a far cry from the real McCoy. The true Buffalo wing is crisp and dry, not saucy, on the outside. The recipe is simplicity itself. A deep fryer is a necessity for great wings. You can bake or grill and then add the wing sauce, but it just is not authentic. Feel free to use fresh or frozen wings.

celery sticks
1/3 cup Butter
blue cheese dressing
2-1/2 pounds chicken wings
1/2 cup Frank's red hot sauce

Heat fryer to 365°F.

Combine hot sauce and butter in a saucepan. Heat at medium low until butter melts, stirring occasionally. Keep sauce hot; it should be thin like melted butter, not like BBQ sauce. If you buy whole wings, cut each wing into three parts separating at the joint, discarding the nubbin. Depending on if the wings are fresh or frozen cooking time will vary. Cook wings a few at a time until crisp on the outside and internal temp is at least 165°F. Remove wings from fryer, let drain and immediately toss in sauce. Remove from sauce. Plate with a garnish of celery sticks and a cup of blue cheese dressing. Repeat until all wings are cooked. Note: you can decrease frying time by baking the wings before frying. Make sure the wings are free of moisture before frying.

Makes about 6 servings.

Allens Hill Farm
Spiced Apple Glazed Lamb Meatballs

1 egg *olive oil*
1 pound ground lamb *salt and pepper to taste*
1 tablespoon fresh parsely *1/2 cup fresh breadcrumbs*
1 tablespoon fresh rosemary *1 tablespoon fresh minced garlic*
1/4 cup Allens Hill Farm Spiced Apple Glaze
Allens Hill Farm Down Under Dukkah (optional) for garnish

Put lamb, breadcrumbs, egg and herbs into bowl. Gently mix until combined. Form into small balls and saute in olive oil over medium heat unitl done. Drain oil and juices from pan and return to low heat. Add glaze to pan and stir until meatballs are coated with glaze. Plate and garnish with dukkah if desired.

Makes 4 to 5 servings.

ALLENS HILL FARM
SMOKEY APPLE GLAZED RIBS

Allens Hill Farm Smokey Apple Glaze
2 racks of ribs (about 3 pounds each rack)

BBQ Rub

2 tablespoons paprika	1 teaspoon black pepper
2 tablespoons kosher salt	2 tablespoons chili powder
2 tablespoons brown sugar	1/4 teaspoon cayenne pepper
1-1/2 teaspoons onion powder	2 tablespoons granulated garlic

Mix together and store unused rub in an airtight container.

Mop Sauce

Ribs are best when they are moist. Sometimes during the cooking process, your ribs might begin to look a bit dry. You can fix this with a good dab of mop sauce.

1/4 cup water
1/2 cup vinegar
1 tablespoon BBQ rub
1 tablespoon Worcestershire sauce

Combine ingredients in a small saucepan. Bring to a boil and let cool. If not using at once, put into a container and refrigerate.

There are several ways to make great ribs. They can of course be cooked right on the grill. You can also make great ribs in the oven. Or you can use a combination of both methods. Whichever way you decide to go, our BBQ rub and Allens Hill Farm Smokey Apple Glaze will make for some of the best ribs you've ever eaten.

If you can find them, go for St. Louie racks. You may have to go to a butcher or a restaurant supplier, but these meaty, uniform racks are great. If not, baby backs or whatever you can find will work.

The first step is to rub down the racks with the BBQ rub. I like to do this as early as the night before to let the flavor penetrate. Sprinkle the ribs liberally with the rub and massage it into the meat until it is completely covered. Cover the racks with plastic wrap until ready to cook.

If cooking your ribs on the grill, charcoal is your best bet. After the coals are ready, push to one side. Place a drip pan with water under the other side. If you want to get real smoked flavor, soak hickory chips in water for at least half an hour, then wrap in aluminum foil packets with holes poked in one side for the smoke to escape. (However, with the Smokey Apple Glaze, this is not really necessary.)

Put the ribs on the grill over the pan of water and cover the grill. You want to keep the temperature about 250°F. Check the ribs every hour or so; if they look dry, dab on (don't brush) some of the mop sauce. Add coals as needed to keep the temperature at about 250°F. The ribs should take about four hours to cook. You can check for doneness a few ways. The most reliable is to use a thermometer. 180°F is your minimum temperature. You can also tell the ribs are ready if they bend easily when you pick them up. If the meat tears easily between the bones, they are ready to go.

The last step is to gently brush on the Allens Hill Farm Smokey Apple Glaze. After that, just let them cook for a few more minutes. If you want the glaze to have a bit of crackle, then flip them over and cook over the coals until they have the color you desire. Take off the grill and let rest for a few minutes so you don't lose all that juiciness you spent those hours to achieve. Cut into portions and enjoy.

This whole process can also be achieved in a 250°F oven (without the wood chips of course). I like to do the cooking in the oven and then finish on the grill. All methods will yield great results.

Makes 6 to 8 servings.

Variation

Allens Hill Farm Apple Cider Molasses is great in place of Smokey Apple Glaze.

Buffalo Party Mix

This is a spicy twist on the original party mix we new as kids. Get creative with the types of cereal, crackers and nuts. I like a sweet, salty, spicy combination. I call this Buffalo party mix since I mix some Frank's hot sauce in with the butter just like wing sauce.

1 cup mini pretzels
3 cups Corn Chex cereal
3 cups Wheat Chex cereal
1 teaspoon seasoned salt
1/2 teaspoon onion powder
1 teaspoon Cajun seasoning
6 tablespoons butter
3 cups Rice Chex cereal
1 teaspoon garlic powder
1 cup honey roasted nuts
1-1/2 cups Goldfish crackers
1 tablespoon Frank's hot sauce
2 tablespoons Worcestershire sauce

Preheat oven to 250°F.

Put butter in a large roasting pan and melt in the oven. Remove pan from oven. Stir in seasonings then add remaining ingredients, stirring gently to coat. Put pan back in oven and bake 1 hour stirring every 15 minutes to make sure all pieces are evenly coated. Spread snack mix onto paper towels until cool. Store in an airtight container.

Makes about 3 quarts.

Pepperoni Dip

This is great for a tailgate or football party. Come to think of it, it's great just about anytime. Make the dip at least a day ahead; the pepperoni flavor becomes better as it sits.

1 pint sour cream
1/2 pound stick of pepperoni
1 large round loaf of fresh rye bread

Put sour cream into a mixing bowl.

Cut pepperoni onto chunks and put into food processor. Chop until medium-fine. Stir pepperoni onto sour cream. Cover and refrigerate at least overnight.

When ready to serve, put bread onto serving plate. Cut out a "bowl" in the top. Take the bread you removed and cut into chunks for dipping and arrange around outside of loaf. Stir dip and put into bread bowl. If desired, garnish with pepperoni slices and parsley.

Caramel Apple Popcorn

Popcorn

Pop popcorn using whatever method you prefer. Air popped is fine, but I like the taste better when using two tablespoons oil (popcorn oil if you have it) and one-half teaspoons salt (popcorn salt is great too). Put into large mixing bowl.

Preheat oven to 225°F.

Caramel Coating

1/2 teaspoon salt
1 cup brown sugar
1/2 teaspoon vanilla
1/2 cup (1 stick) butter
1/2 teaspoon baking soda
1/2 cup Allens Hill Farm Apple Cider Molasses

Place sugar, molasses, butter and salt into a heavy saucepan. Cook over medium heat until it comes to a boil. Reduce heat to keep a nice steady boil going and continue to cook for five minutes.

Remove from heat and add vanilla and soda and stir until foamy. Pour over popped corn and stir until well coated. Bake for 90 minutes stirring every 15 minutes. When done, dump onto baking sheets to cool. Store in an airtight container.

Makes about 3 to 4 quarts.

Carnival Fried Dough

I know, it's too simple to include as a recipe, but we never think to make some. It's fun and simple. Why pay a crazy price at a local carnival when you can make it for pennies at home anytime.

1 recipe pizza dough
granulated sugar, for dusting

Preheat oil in a deep fryer to 375°F. Cut off a hunk of dough about the size of a lemon. Flatten and stretch out until quite thin, say one-eighth of an inch. Gently lay into oil. If bubbles and domes form, press down with tongs. When the bottom is golden brown, flip over and cook until the other side is as well. Remove from oil, drain on absorbent paper and immediately sprinkle generously with sugar. Eat at once.

Makes 6 to 8 servings.

Cajun Dipping Sauce

1 cup sour cream
1 cup mayonnaise
2 teaspoons Cajun seasoning (more or less to taste)
1/4–1/2 teaspoon Tabasco sauce (more or less to taste)

Put ingredients in bowl and mix together. Cover and refrigerate for a few hours to flavor through. Adjust seasonings to taste. Use as a dip for chips, veggies or fries. It's also great as condiment for chicken fingers, fish or as a spread on a sandwich or wrap.

Makes 1 pint.

Sweet Potato Chips

If you want to impress someone with a snack that is incredibly simple to make, fry up some of these. The combination of the natural sweetness of the potato with the bite of salt and crisp crunch is absolutely addictive.

Fine sea salt
One sweet potato or yam per person

Scrub and dry sweet potatoes. Do not peel. Slice very thin, use a mandolin if you have one. Place sliced potatoes in a bowl of ice water until ready to cook. Heat oil in pan or fryer to 375°F. Remove potatoes from water and dry with paper towels. Put dried slices into fryer. Do not overload to avoid depressing oil temperature. Stir frequently to insure even cooking. When chips become crisp, remove from fryer and drain on absorbent paper. Immediately sprinkle with salt. Great hot or cold. Excellent with Cajun dipping sauce.

Pizza

If you want to make pizza at home that is better (and much less expensive) than you can get at a pizzeria, there are a couple of important things to do.

First, you need a hot (450°F) oven and a baking stone. If you don't have one, you can make one economically. Measure your oven rack and deduct an inch on each side to allow for heat and air circulation. Go to a home improvement store and get unglazed quarry tile that are used for floor tiles. If you don't have a way to cut them yourself, they can cut them for you. Bring them home, wash and let dry. Then lay on your oven rack. You now have the equivalent of the deck of a pizza oven at home. You will also need a peel to slide the pizza on to and off the stone. You can order on line, go to a restaurant supply, or if cheap like me, make one from a quarter-inch thick piece of plywood.

Next, you need good ingredients. Fresh pizza dough is a must! Use the recipe on page 142. You can spend as much on cheese as you like, but a low-moisture, part skim mozzarella works well. Always mix in some grated parmesan to keep it from clumping and to add flavor. When I top with veggies, I like to lightly sauté them first in some olive oil. This brings out flavor and drives out some moisture preventing a soggy pizza. Find a commercial pizza sauce you like or use olive oil. I think pizza is incomplete without a liberal dose of oregano and occasionally some red pepper flakes.

When forming the crust remember to pull, not press. If you roll out the dough, you will destroy all of the wonderful bubbles you have created. Pull, stretch or if you are adventurous, toss and spin.

Pizza is a blank canvas. Be creative and have fun!

Traditional Pizza

oregano
1 jar of pizza sauce
1/3 cup grated parmesan
1 pound shredded mozzarella
assorted toppings of your choice
1 batch Italian bread dough (recipe on page 142)

Preheat oven with stone to 450°F.

Sprinkle cornmeal on peel to prevent sticking.

Flour work surface and shape crust. (You can make a sheet pizza by pressing dough into a sheet pans coated with olive oil) or a deep dish "pan" pizza using a large cast iron skillet).

Slide crust onto peel. Spread on pizza sauce or olive oil. Top with cheese. Sprinkle on oregano. Add toppings. Slide onto pizza stone.

Bake 8-10 minutes until crust is done and cheese is melted. Remove from oven. Let rest for a minute to allow cheese to set and cut.

Makes 1 pizza (serves 4 to 6).

Bruschetta Pizza

I make this for a change of pace, especially when it's farm market season in the summer, or when I'm on a diet. It's light, flavorful and much lower in fat and calories than a conventional pizza.

The problem with vegetable pizzas is that they can get soggy from all of the moisture from the vegetables. I have a trick to fix that.

Since cheese is not the base of the pizza toppings but a flavoring, get very good quality parmesan to freshly grate over the top.

3 garlic cloves
1/4 cup olive oil
6 medium mushrooms
2 teaspoon kosher or sea salt
1/4 cup chopped fresh parsley
1 green pepper
3 medium tomatoes
1/2 teaspoon dried oregano
1 small bunch of green onions
1/4 teaspoon red pepper flakes
1 ounce block of parmesan to grate
1 recipe Italian bread dough (recipe on page 142)

Wash vegetables. Halve the tomatoes and remove seeds and chop. Place into mixing bowl. Slice peppers and mushrooms very thin and add to bowl. Slice green onions, including the green part and add. Mash garlic cloves with 1 teaspoons salt. Let sit for a minute then add to other vegetables.

Add remaining herbs, salt and 2 tablespoons of olive oil. Toss together and let sit for at least an hour to macerate. Pour veggies into a fine meshed strainer and let drain.

Preheat oven with stone to 450°F.

Sprinkle cornmeal on peel to prevent sticking. Flour work surface and shape crust. Slide crust onto peel. Spread on 2 tablespoons of olive oil.

Dump vegetbles into a piece of cheesecloth or several paper towels and gently squeeze out additional moisture. Strew over crust. Grate parmesan over the top. Slide onto pizza stone.

Bake 8-10 minutes until crust is done and cheese is melted. Remove from oven.

Makes 1 pizza (serves 4 to 6).

Let's Talk Finger Lakes Wines & Cheese

The Finger Lakes region of New York State has been an agricultural center since it was originally settled in the late 1700's. Wines have been produced here for decades, but in the last 30 years, the local wine industry has exploded. Where a handful of wineries once existed, dozens are now in operation with more opening each year.

Although quality is improving dramatically, there is a wide deviation between the excellent and mediocre. Many wineries are rich retiree's playgrounds, some are meant to attract the hordes of vino-tourists who roam the region. Still, there are some truly dedicated and gifted vintners who are producing world class wines, especially Chardonnay. I'll give you a few of my personal favorites, but by all means, explore and taste and find your own favorites.

Keuka Lake

Heron Hill Winery
9301 County Road 76, Hammondsport, NY 14840
   Renowned late harvest and ice wines, reds and whites.

Bully Hill Vineyards
8843 Greyton H. Taylor Memorial Dr., Hammondsport, New York 14840
   One of the pioneer wineries in the Finger Lakes, Bully Hill produces a wide variety of varietals and blends with the most interesting and artistic labels anywhere.

Dr. Konstantin Frank Vinifera Wine Cellars
9749 Middle Road, Hammondsport, NY 14840

Dr. Frank was a pioneer in introducing the Old World vinifera grapes to the United States. His family produces some of the finest wines and champagnes not only in the Finger Lakes but in the United States.

Ravines Wine Cellars
14630 State Route 54 Hammondsport, NY 14840

A boutique winery, Ravines in owned by a trained European winemaker who produces some of the finest reds in the area.

Seneca Lake

Fox Run Vineyards
670 State Route 14, Penn Yan, New York 14527

Excellent red and white varietals and ports.

Wagner Vineyards
9322 State Route 414, Lodi, New York 14860

Estate-bottled wines and handcrafted beers from Wagner Valley Brewing.

Chateau Lafayette Reneau
5081 State Route 414, Hector, New York 14841

Award winning Riesling, chardonnay, pinot noir, cabernet and merlot.

Glenora Wine Cellars
5435 State Route 14, Dundee, New York 14837

The oldest winery on Seneca Lake, Glenora produces a wide variety of whites, reds, dessert and sparkling wines.

Anthony Road Wine Company
1020 Anthony Road, Penn Yan, New York 14527

An array of wines, from dry to dessert, with a range of tastes designed to please connoisseurs and casual aficionados alike.

Hermann J. Wiemer Vineyard

3962 Rte. 14, Starkey, NY 14837

Hermann J. Wiemer is regarded as one of the pioneers of viticulture and winemaking in the Finger Lakes region. Estate grown and bottled wines have a nationwide reputation for being exceptionally lush, crisp and well-balanced.

Cayuga Lake

Sheldrake Point Winery

7448 County Road 153, Ovid, NY 14521

Quality premium varietals including Cabernet Franc, Riesling, Gewurztraminer, Pinot Gris, Pinot Noir, Gamay, Merlot, Cabernet Sauvignon and Chardonnay.

Six Mile Creek Vineyard

1551 Slaterville Road, Ithaca, NY

Six Mile Creek reds are typically medium bodied. In addition to very good Riesling and Chardonnay, they are known for flavorful and zesty wines produced from hybrid grapes. Distilled specialties bottled under the family name, Spirits by Battistella, includes the first wine based Vodka in the Finger Lakes, as well as some Italian specialties.

Swedish Hill Vineyards

4565 Rt. 414 , Romulus, NY 14541

Cayuga Lake's largest selection of wines, ranging from dry to sweet, classic to unique, and including Sparkling Wines, Port, and Brandy.

Goose Watch Winery

5480 Route 89, Romulus, NY 14541

Premium Pinot Grigio, Traminette, Viognier, Merlot and White Port, Sherry and Ice Wines. Seasonal farm-raised chestnuts.

Lucas Vineyards

3862 County Road 150, Interlaken, NY 14847

Cayuga Lake's oldest winery; nautical-inspired "Tug Boat" and "Nautie" Vinifera and Methode Champenoise Sparkling Wines.

In the last few years, a number of truly excellent cheese makers have been producing a wide variety of cheese throughout the area using local milks. My favorites are:

Finger Lakes Farmstead Cheese Co.
5491 Bergen Rd., Trumansburg, NY 14886

Producing European style farmstead cheeses including gouda and gruyere style cheeses.

Murano Cheese Co.
3075 Rt. 96, Waterloo, NY 13165

Aged, hand-made cheeses including Colby and raw milk cheddar.

Sunset View Creamery
4970 County Rd. 14, Odessa, New York 14869

Several varieties of Monterey Jack and Cheddars aged up to 5 years.

Lively Run Goat Dairy
8978 County Rd 142, Interlaken NY 14847

Goat milk cheeses including Feta, French style Chevre, and Blue.

Pantry Checklist

🌿 I'm going to give you a quick list of some of the items I like to keep on hand either in the freezer, fridge or pantry.

It's important to keep a well-stocked kitchen; you don't want to have to run to the store before every meal. It also helps you to exercise more creativity.

You don't need a lot of everything, but if you can store it and afford it, buying in bulk can save you a lot of cash. The list and recipes on the following pages can make a convenient shopping list.

Pantry Recipes

GRILL SEASONING

1/4 cup seasoned salt
1/4 cup ground black pepper

Mix and store in a shaker can.

BBQ RUB

2 tablespoons paprika
2 tablespoons kosher salt
2 tablespoons brown sugar
1-1/2 teaspoons onion powder
1 teaspoon black pepper
2 tablespoons chili powder
1/4 teaspoon cayenne pepper
2 tablespoons granulated garlic

Mix together and store unused rub in an airtight container.

FRENCH APPLE DRESSING AND MARINADE

1/2 cup apple cider
1/2 cup vegatable oil
salt and pepper to taste
2 pieces crystallized ginger
1/2 teaspoon allspice
1/2 teaspoon cinnamon
2 tablespoons lemon juice
1 teaspoons fresh minced garlic
1 cup Allens Hill Farm Apple Cider Molasses
1/4 cup assorted fresh herbs – chives, parsley

Place all ingredients except oil in a blender or food processor and blend until smooth. Continue to blend while slowly adding oil. Add salt and pepper to taste. Also makes a great marinade

CROUTONS

salt
1 teaspoon garlic powder
1/2 teaspoon parsley flakes
4 tablespoon butter or margarine
4 slices of bread or leftover buns, rolls

Cut the bread into one-inch squares. Melt the butter in a skillet over medium high heat. Add bread and stir or toss to coat with butter. Sprinkle with garlic powder, parsley and a little salt. Cook, stirring frequently until croutons are lightly browned and crunchy.

CAJUN DIPPING SAUCE

1 cup sour cream
1 cup mayonnaise
2 teaspoons Cajun seasoning (more or less to taste)
1/4–1/2 teaspoon Tabasco sauce (more or less to taste)

Put ingredients in bowl and mix together. Cover and refrigerate for a few hours to flavor through. Adjust seasonings to taste. Use as a dip for chips, veggies or fries. It's also great as condiment for chicken fingers, fish or as a spread on a sandwich or wrap.

Makes 1 pint.

The Allens Hill Farm Cookbook

Pantry List

Herbs & Spices

salt: table salt, sea salt. Kosher salt, seasoned salt
pepper: ground pepper, whole peppercorns

basil	cumin
cinnamon	nutmeg
ginger	cloves
allspice	thyme
marjoram	parsley
oregano	bay leaf
cayenne	garlic powder
chili powder	fennel seeds
caraway seeds	rubbed sage
sesame seeds	poppy seeds

red pepper flakes

Meat

beef: hamburger, steaks, roast, stew
chicken: boneless breasts, whole chicken, wings or other preferred parts
pork: chops, roast
sausage: hot dogs, smoked, breakfast, Italian

Condiments

ketchup	mustard
soy sauce	BBQ sauce
mayonnaise	lemon juice
steak sauce	salad dressings

Worcestershire sauce

Dry Goods

vanilla raisins
cornmeal baking soda
baking powder vegetable oil
cocoa powder chocolate chips
baking chocolate evaporated milk
condensed milk tomato paste
canned tomatoes vegetable shortening
beef and chicken base non-stick cooking spray
flour; bread, all purpose and pastry
buttermilk powder
vinegar: apple cider, red wine, balsamic
sugar; granulated, confectioner's, light brown
Allens Hill Farm Apple Cider Molasses
Allens Hill Farm Smokey Apple Glaze
Allens Hill Farm Spices Apple Glaze

Dairy

milk
butter
cheese: cheddar, mozzarella, provolone, parmesan, Swiss, American slices

Produce

garlic onions
celery carrots
limes lemons
oranges potatoes
tomatoes cucumbers
mushrooms salad greens
green peppers

Ingredient Suppliers: Lets Talk Local

I can give you a dozen good reasons to buy locally produced products: quality, value, supporting local farmers and businesses, etc. I'll give you some good sources if you live in my area. If not, begin scouting your own sources. Some ingredients can't be locally sourced, so I'll give you some of my favorites.

Check these suppliers' websites to find outlets, farm markets and on line ordering.

Finger Lakes Culinary Bounty is an excellent resource to find all kinds of local products and restaurants who are committed to using local products: **www.flcb.org**.

Allens Hill Farm

3663 County Road 40
Bloomfield, NY 14469
585-657-4710
www.allenshillfarm.com
info@allenshillfarm.com

Allens Hill Farm is a producer of all natural specialty food products including apple cider molasses, syrups and glazes; cookie, cake, pancake, bread and muffin mixes, dukkah, granola and snack bars.

Meats/Poultry

Whitney Farms
David & Judy Whitney
3820 Fowlerville Road, Avon, NY 14414 • 585-690-0784; 585-690-0772
www.whitneyfarmsny.com

NOFA certified organic grass fed beef and pork.

Aberdeen Hill Farm
P.O. Box 161, Gorham, NY 14461
www.aberdeenhillfarm.com

Grass fed pork, beef and lamb

Honeyhill Farm
6241 Price Road, Livonia, NY 14487-9523
www.honeyhillorganicfarm.com

Certified organic pastured chicken, beef, garlic, heirloom tomatoes.

Produce

Organic Matters Farm
1979 Shuler Road, Lyons, NY 14489 • 315-331-8319

    Organic produce and eggs.

Red Jacket Orchards
957 Routes 5&20, Geneva, NY 14456 • 800-828-9410; 315-781-2749
www.redjacketorchards.com

    Apples, fruits, vegetables and juices.

Freshwise Farms
1345 Penfield Center Road, Penfield, NY • 585-872-7303
www.freshwise.com

    Hydroponic and field-grown greens and vegetables.

Gale-Wyn Farm
Fisher Hill Road, Canandaigua, NY 14424• 585-657-7752

    A wide variety of produce.

Honey

Bloomfield Honey Farm
8828 Belcher Road, Bloomfield, NY 14469• 585-229-2236
www.bloomfieldhoney.com

    Raw honey, candles, bee keeping supplies and cosmetics.

Eggs

Nordic Farms
3326 Parker Road, Branchport, NY 14418• 315-595-8803
www.nordicfarmjams.com

    Jams, jellies, fresh eggs

Coffee

Joe Bean Coffee Roasters
182 North Avenue, Webster, NY 14580 • 585-265-4710
www.joebeancoffee.com

    Artisan roasted organic and fair trades coffee.

Baking Supplies

New Hope Mills
181 York Street, Auburn, NY 13021 • 315-252-2676
www.newhopemills.com

    Pancake mixes, flours, bulk baking supplies.

Birkett Mills
163 Main Street, Penn Yan, NY 14527 • 315-536-3311
www.thebirkettmills.com

    Millers of buckwheat and soft wheat flours, pancake mixes.

Spices

Mountain Rose Herbs
PO Box 50220, Eugene, OR 97405 • 800-879-3337
www.mountainroseherbs.com

    Organic herbs and spices.

Saltworks
Woodinville, WA 98072 • 800-355-7258
www.saltworks.us

    Every imaginable variety of salt.

Recipe Index

Appetizers/Snacks
- Buffalo Party Mix — 166
- Buffalo Wings — 164
- Cajun Dipping Sauce — 168
- Caramel Apple Popcorn — 167
- Crudités — 110
- Dukkah — 160
- Dukkah Wings — 163
- Pepperoni Dip — 167
- Smokey Apple Glazed Ribs — 165
- Sweet and Spicy Wings — 163
- Sweet Potato Chips — 168

Apple Cider Molasses — 13
- Apple Cider Molasses Cornbread — 146
- Apple Cider Molasses Gingerbread — 151
- Aunt Mildred's Camp Cookies — 153
- Baked Beans — 115
- Caramel Apple Popcorn — 167
- Allens Hill Farm Corn Muffins — 127
- Easy Non-Fat Whole Wheat Bread — 146
- French Apple Dressing and Marinade — 176
- Grandma's Molasses Cookies — 153
- Granola — 40
- Spice Cake — 150
- Pork with Apple Onion Glaze — 98

Apple
- See: apple cider molasses
- Apple Oatmeal Crumble — 157
- Applesauce Muffins — 128
- Applesauce — 116
- Pork with Apple Onion Glaze — 98
- French Apple Dressing and Marinade — 176
- Baked Pork Chops with Stuffing — 75
- Quick Apple Shortcake — 134

Bacon — 47
- Bacon Wrapped Green Beans — 112
- Canadian Bacon — 47
- Finger Lakes Locavore Quiche — 100

Barbeque
- BBQ Rub — 176
- See Grilling — 84

Beans
- Bacon Wrapped Green Beans — 112
- Baked Beans — 115

Beef
- Chili Con Carne — 65
- Cincinnati Chili — 66
- Grilled Marinated Steak — 84
- Herb Crusted Roast Beef — 97
- Meatballs — 57
- Meatloaf — 76
- Patty Melt — 50
- Pot Roast — 69
- Quick Beef Stew — 61
- Stew — 63
- Southwest Chili — 66

Biscuits
- Baking Powder Biscuits — 133
- Buttermilk Biscuits — 132
- Cinnamon Raisin Biscuits — 133
- Garlic Cheese Biscuits — 147

Bread: Yeasted Breads
- Basic Sweet Bread Dough — 139
- Beignets — 137
- Carnival Fried Dough — 168
- Cheddar Twist Bread — 144

The Allens Hill Farm Cookbook

Country Fair Egg Bread	143	Canadian Bacon	47
Dinner Rolls	140	Caramel Apple Popcorn	167
English Muffins	131	Carnival Fried Dough	168
Garlic Bread Sticks	142		
Kuchen	123	Casseroles	
Italian Bread Dough	142	Ed's Favorite Mac and Cheese	70
Italian Bread	143	Twice Baked Potato Casserole	105
Mike's Favorite Cinnamon Buns	118	Jambalaya	67
Orange Rolls	141	Scalloped Potatoes and Ham	72
Swiss Braid	140		
Yeast Raised Doughnuts	135	Cereals	
		Cornmeal Mush	40
Bread: Quick Breads		Granola	40
See Scone	129	Oatmeal	39
See muffins			
See biscuits		Cheese	
Corn Bread	146	Ed's Favorite Mac and Cheese	70
Easy Non-Fat Whole Wheat Bread	146	Local	173
Irish Soda Bread	145		
Real Garlic Bread	108	Chicken	
		Baked Chicken Parts	77
Breakfast Sandwiches	45	Boneless Chicken and Rice	59
		Buffalo Wings	164
Brownies		Chicken and Stuffing	78
Black Forest Brownie Sundae	157	Chicken Parmesan	80
Brownie Pecan Pie	158	Classic Roasted Chicken	92
		Dukkah Wings	163
Buttermilk		Dukkah Stuffed Chicken Breasts	95
Buttermilk Biscuits	132	Grilled Chicken Breasts	87
Buttermilk Doughnuts	137	Grilled Chicken with Cornell Marinade	87
Buttermilk Muffins with Topping	126	Oven Fried Chicken	79
Buttermilk Pancakes	33	Potato Crusted Chicken Breasts	93
		Sautéed Chicken Breasts	78
Cajun Dipping Sauce	168	Smokey Glazed BBQ Chicken	86
		Stuffed Chicken Breasts	96
Cake			
Apple Cider Molasses Gingerbread	151	Chili	
Cholesterol-Free Chocolate Cake	149	Cincinnati Chili	66
Pound Cake	150	Chili Con Carne	65
Quick Apple Shortcake	134	Southwest Chili	66
Quick Crumb Coffee Cake	120		
Sour Cream Coffee Cake	122		

The Allens Hill Farm Cookbook

Chocolate
    Cholesterol-Free Chocolate Cake   149

Cinnamon
    Cinnamon Baked Apples   158
    Cinnamon Raisin Biscuits   133
    Cinnamon Raisin Bread   141
    Mike's Favorite Cinnamon Buns   118

Coffee Cakes
    Kuchen   123
    Quick Crumb Coffee Cake   120
    Sour Cream Coffee Cake   122

Cookies
    Aunt Mildred's Camp Cookies   153
    Big Chewy Chocolate Chip Cookies   152
    Wheat-Free Oatmeal Cookies   155
    Katherine's Date Cookies   155
    Mom's Peanut Butter Cookies   154
    Soft Sugar Cookies   156

Corn   112
Corn Bread   146
Corn Muffins   127
Cornell Marinade   87

Cornmeal
    Corn Bread   146
    Corn Muffins   127
    Cornmeal Mush   40
    Cornmeal Pancakes   34

Cornish Game Hens with Stuffing   95

Crepes   36
Crepes with Eggs   37
Crepes with Fresh Greens   100

Croutons   177
Crudités   110

Desserts
    See cakes, cookies, brownies
    Cinnamon Baked Apples   158

Dips
    Cajun Dipping Sauce   168
    Pepperoni Dip   167

Doughnuts
    Beignets   137
    Buttermilk Doughnuts   137
    Yeast Raised Doughnuts   135

Dressings/marinades
    Cajun Dipping Sauce   168
    Cornell Marinade   87
    French Apple Dressing and Marinade   176

Dukkah   160
    Dukkah Broiled Fish   82
    Dukkah Stuffed Chicken Breasts   95
    Dukkah Wings   163
    Grilled Tomatoes with Dukkah   113

Eggs
    Breakfast Sandwiches   45
    Crepes with Eggs   37
    Fried Eggs   42
    Hard Boiled Eggs   42
    My Late Night Omelet   44
    Omelets   43
    Poached Eggs   42
    Scrambled Eggs   43
    Soft Boiled Eggs   42

English Muffins   131

Fish
    Beer Batter Fish Fry   82
    Broiled Fish Fillet   81
    Dukkah Broiled Fish   82
    Grilled Salmon with Glaze   99
    Oven-fried Fish   81

The Allens Hill Farm Cookbook

French Apple Dressing and Marinade	176
French Toast	38
Fried Cornmeal Mush	40
Fried Rice	59
Garbage Plate™	49

Garlic
Garlic Bread Sticks	142
Garlic Cheese Biscuits	147
Real Garlic Bread	108

Granola	40

Grill
Grill Seasoning	176
Grilled Chicken Breasts	87
Grilled Chicken with Cornell Marinade	87
Grilled Lamb Chops	97
Grilled Marinated Steak	84
Grilled Salmon with Glaze	99
Grilled Tomatoes with Dukkah	113

Ham
Baked Ham with Spiced Apple Glaze	99
Scalloped Potatoes and Ham	72

Hash Browns	47
Home Fries	46
Irish Soda Bread	145
Italian Bread Dough	142
Italian Bread	143
Jambalaya	67
Kuchen	123

Lamb
Grilled Lamb Chops	97
Spiced Apple Glazed Lamb Meatballs	164

Meatballs	57
Meatloaf	76

Muffins
Bran Muffins	127
Buttermilk Muffins with Topping	126
Corn Muffins	127
Simple Buttermilk Muffins	126
Simple Muffins	125

Mushrooms	112

Oatmeal
Oatmeal Muffins	128
Oatmeal	39

Omelets see eggs	
Orange Rolls	141

Pancakes/Waffles
	32
Buttermilk Pancakes	33
Belgian Waffles	38
Cornmeal Pancakes	34
Crepes	36
Crepes with Eggs	37
French Toast	38
Mom's Golden Waffles	37
Old Fashioned Buckwheat Cakes	36
Sourdough Pancakes	34

Pasta
Baked Ziti	71
Skillet Pasta	56

Patty Melt	50
Pepperoni Dip	167

Pizza
Bruschetta Pizza	170
Ten Minute Pizza	51
Traditional Pizza	170

Pork	
Baked Pork Chops with Stuffing	75
Breaded Pork Chops	74
Smokey Apple Glazed Ribs	165
Pan Fried Pork Chops	73
Pork with Apple Onion Glaze	98
Also see ham	

Potato	
Baked Potato	105
Herb Roasted Potatoes	104
Hash Browns	47
Home Fries	46
Oven Fries	104
Twice Baked Potato Casserole	105
Potato Crusted Chicken Breasts	93
Sweet Potato Chips	168
Smashed Potatoes	106

Poultry	
See chicken	
Cornish Game Hens with Stuffing	95
Turkey with Sausage Stuffing	94

Pound Cake	150

Quiche	
Finger Lakes Locavore Quiche	100

Rolls see bread yeasted and biscuits

Salad	89, 114
Sausage	47
Sausage, Peppers and Onions	68

Scone	
Basic Scone	129
Oatmeal Raisin Scone	130

Soup	
Super Simple Soup	60

Stew	63
Quick Beef Stew	61

Stir Fry	61
Red Neck Stir Fry	58

Stuffing	108
Turkey with Sausage Stuffing	94

Waffles: see Pancakes/Waffles

Vegetables	
See potatoes	110
Grilled Tomatoes with Dukkah	113
Bacon Wrapped Green Beans	112
Mushrooms	112
Winter Squash	111
Zucchini	111

Yogurt Parfait	48

Made in the USA
Lexington, KY
07 June 2010